IMAGES
of America

UPTOWN
MINNEAPOLIS

(Courtesy Minneapolis Public Library.)

IMAGES
of America

UPTOWN
MINNEAPOLIS

Thatcher Imboden and Cedar Imboden Phillips

ARCADIA
PUBLISHING

Published by Arcadia Publishing
Charleston, South Carolina

Library of Congress Catalog Card Number: 2004112447

For all general information contact Arcadia Publishing at:
Telephone 843-853-2070
Fax 843-853-0044
E-mail sales@arcadiapublishing.com
For customer service and orders:
Toll-Free 1-888-313-2665

Visit us on the Internet at www.arcadiapublishing.com

(Courtesy Thatcher Imboden.)

CONTENTS

ACKNOWLEDGMENTS

Compiling a book of this nature required the help of many individuals. We wanted to use photographs drawn from the best of both private and public collections, and are grateful for the assistance and generosity of so many people, organizations, and businesses. The following people made this book into a reality and we could not have done it without their help. The staff at the Hennepin History Museum, with special thanks to Todd Mahon, Susan Larson-Fleming, and Jack Kabrud, allowed us access to their exhaustive photo archives. Similarly, the friendly and ever-helpful members of the Minneapolis Public Library's Special Collections department deserve special thanks, especially librarians JoEllen Haugo and Wendy Adamson. Photographs also come from the collections of both the Minnesota Historical Society and the Smithsonian American Art Museum. Local businesses, organizations, and individuals were generous with their time and photographs. Michael Legeros, an Arcadia author himself, helped us with photos, research, and general advice. Charles "Zeke" Koehler provided photographs and memories, as did Clarence Nelson. We would also like to thank, in no particular order, William Morton, Joyce United Methodist Church, the Brave New Workshop, Barbara Lee, Tres Lund, Lunds Foods, Alison Lindburg, Michael Lander, Scott Engel, Tania Fritz, Warner Properties, Cindy Fitzpatrick, the Uptown Association, Steve Granger, the Minneapolis Park and Recreation Board, the Facilities Department of the Minneapolis Public Schools, Neal Frank, Temple Israel, John Legeros, Terry and Tom Olson, Mary Ann Knox, Patricia Pennington Idstrom, Tian Barbatsis Dayton, Barbara Brooks, Dick Lindskoog, the Extra Alarm Association of the Twin Cities, Meg Tuthill, Joseph Melzer, and Tom Neiman. Our editor Maura Brown was a great help from start to finish. Our parents, Durant and Cheryl Imboden, and brother Anders were always enthusiastic and encouraging. Thatcher would also like to thank Melissa Kusmich for her support as well as technical assistance. Cedar wants to thank her husband Andrew for his steady encouragement and patience.

INTRODUCTION

"Everybody's going to Uptown, that's where I wanna be." —*Prince*

Uptown, in the words of Minneapolis native and former Uptown business owner Prince, may be where you want to be, but where exactly *is* Uptown? Uptown as an area does not have distinct boundaries, and the definition of what constitutes Uptown depends on who you ask. The division between what is Lyn-Lake and what is Uptown, for example, is debatable. For the purpose of this book, Uptown consists of the four neighborhoods surrounding the Hennepin and Lake business core. These neighborhoods—CARAG, ECCO, Lowry Hill East (the Wedge), and East Isles—each have their own distinct character but have developed an overall Uptown identity. We further narrowed our definition of Uptown by focusing on the Hennepin-Lake intersection and the neighborhoods radiating out from that core, with rough boundaries of 36th Street to the south, 22nd Street to the north, Lake Calhoun and Lake of the Isles to the west, and Bryant Avenue to the east.

Uptown has not always been called Uptown. In its earliest years, the area was known primarily for its lakes. Attention began to shift from the lakes to the Hennepin-Lake intersection as it grew to become one of the city's strongest business districts outside of downtown. The earliest origins of the name "Uptown" date to the late 1920s. In April of 1929, the *Minneapolis Journal* announced the name change of a well-known local theater. "Effective next Thursday," the paper reported, "Finkelstein and Ruben's Lagoon Theater will be known as the Uptown Theater." The name change, they added, was to "conform with a movement now in progress to establish the Lake and Hennepin community as 'The Uptown District of Minneapolis.'" The inspiration for the name came from the "famous and prosperous" Uptown district of Chicago. By the 1930s, stores using "Uptown" in their names were operating in the area, and the local business association had become the Uptown Business Association.

Despite the early attempts to create a name and identity for the Hennepin-Lake business district, most locals still thought of the commercial core as Hennepin and Lake. Uptown continued to be used in the names of businesses, organizations, and events, but never caught on as a general identifier of the area. It was not until the early 1980s, around the time of the development of Calhoun Square, that Uptown began to be used by the general public as the name for the commercial district and its surrounding areas.

The Hennepin-Lake intersection is the heart of Uptown. Starting in the 1920s, this busy intersection has historically been home to some of Minneapolis's most famous restaurants, nightclubs, businesses, and events. For years, people from around the region flocked to Hennepin and Lake's Rainbow Café, a local institution. Residents visited the Granada Theater, the Uptown Theater, and the Calhoun Theater to see vaudeville shows and films. Ballrooms and nightclubs attracted those in search of further evening entertainment. At the nearby Minneapolis Arena, located at Dupont and 29th Street, locals could watch a minor league hockey game, take in an Ice Follies show, roller skate to organ music during the summer, or dance on the emptied ice surface to a 17-piece orchestra in what was billed the country's largest ballroom.

The 1980s were another milestone decade in Uptown's history. After Calhoun School was demolished in 1974, developer Ray Harris began to dream of the possibilities that existed in the empty site one block off of Hennepin and Lake. The struggle to build Calhoun Square, a shopping complex adapting existing buildings into one large structure, was a source of ongoing controversy until the end of the decade. Opponents to the project feared the suburbanization of the area, derisively calling the project "Updale." Despite the critic's arguments, the Minneapolis City Council signaled their support by voting to designate the area "blighted" in order to secure bond financing for the project. Calhoun Square finally opened in 1984 and ushered in a new era for Uptown. Today, Uptown's commercial core still offers a broad range of unique stores, as well as one of the largest selections of nightlife options in the city. Long-time stores such as Lunds and Morris and Christie's continue to serve local residents, while new businesses move in with hopes of becoming area institutions themselves. In addition to its commercial offerings, Uptown also has an industrial heritage. The railroad tracks on 29th Street connected area manufacturers and industry to the greater city, region, and nation. Ice companies pulled ice from Lake Calhoun and stored it in ice houses lining 29th Street. Lumberyards, coal yards, dairies, and stables all called Uptown home. The Buzza Greeting Card Company set up their headquarters in the impressive Buzza Building on Lake Street.

The industrial and commercial centers of Uptown were surrounded by residential neighborhoods, providing homes for both the city's wealthiest citizens as well as its working classes. Large apartment buildings lined parts of Hennepin Avenue, while the neighborhood surrounding Lake of the Isles filled with large houses and mansions. From the historic mansions of Minneapolis millionaires to small arts and crafts bungalows to Moorish-style 1920s apartment buildings, the Uptown area offered something for everyone. Small neighborhood stores, predominately pharmacies, grocery stores, meat markets, and barbers and beauty salons, were scattered throughout Uptown's residential streets, often nestled in the basements of neighborhood apartment buildings.

Uptown's schools have historically been at the heart of the community, although only one now remains. For much of the twentieth century, students could spend their entire educational career in the area. They began school at Calhoun Elementary School on Lake Street and Girard. Once they reached seventh grade they moved further down Hennepin Avenue to Jefferson Junior High. West High School, also on Hennepin Avenue, served local residents from 1909 until its closing in 1982. The closings of both West and Calhoun, as well as the movement towards busing and magnet schools, has changed the character of the neighborhood.

Today, Uptown continues to be a vibrant place for a diverse mix of Minneapolis residents to live, work, and play. An extensive bus network connects the area with the rest of the Twin Cities, just as the streetcars did earlier in the twentieth century. Lakes Calhoun and Isles continue to draw visitors. While some things have changed—the lack of a local high school, the closing of the local post office and police station—others remain the same. Most residents and visitors would agree with Prince—Uptown, it's where you want to be.

One

DEVELOPMENT
AND THE LAKES

Uptown's lakes, Lake Calhoun in particular, have always attracted residents and visitors. Local Dakota called the eastern shore of Lake Calhoun home during the 1830s. Later in the century the lake became a popular tourist destination. "The lake abounds in fish and is a favorite pleasure ground for the officers of Fort Snelling," wrote an 1851 visitor. "The lakes possessed every desirable advantage besides beauty," wrote another nineteenth-century observer, "they were not only full of the finest fish, but in the adjacent woodlands every kind of game abounded, and a great variety of wild fruits grew in profusion." By the 1870s, large resort hotels had developed along the shores of Lake Calhoun. Streetcars made the lakes and their attractions easily accessible to people from across the Twin Cities.

In 1883 the recently-formed Minneapolis Park Board began actively purchasing the land ringing the lakes. Over the course of several decades, they completed a series of ambitious dredging projects that created new shorelines with beaches for Lake Calhoun and a dramatic makeover removing swamps and two islands in Lake of the Isles. Today, Lakes Calhoun and Isles are integral parts of the city's urban park system. Although their shapes and forms have been drastically altered over the years, Lake Calhoun and Lake of the Isles retain their long-time appeal to residents and visitors alike.

The Dakota village of Eatonville, located on the eastern shore of Lake Calhoun, was established in 1829 with the cooperation of Dakota chief Cloudman and Fort Snelling's Indian Agent, Major Taliaferno. The United States was actively encouraging local Indian tribes to shift to an agricultural lifestyle, and the federal government provided Cloudman's village with goods and assistance. Not all local Dakota approved of the village, and Eatonville was established with only 12 families. Several years later the village's population reached 125 and its residents had raised nearly 1,000 bushels of corn. Shown here is the village in the summer of 1835, as painted by artist George Catlin. The village was abandoned in 1839 after local Dakota and Chippewa tensions erupted in violence. (Courtesy Smithsonian American Art Museum, Gift of Mrs. Joseph Harrison Jr.)

Brothers Gideon and Samuel Pond, originally from Connecticut, came to Minnesota in 1834 in search of potential converts to Christianity. They received permission from Fort Snelling's Major Taliaferno to live near the village of Eatonville on the eastern shore of Lake Calhoun. Neither brother had formal religious training, nor knowledge of the Dakota language or customs. They quickly set to work learning the Dakota language, developing an alphabet so that Biblical works could be translated and published in the language. Both brothers later wrote prolifically about their experiences living with the Dakota. Shown here is Gideon Pond. (Courtesy Hennepin History Museum.)

The Ponds' cabin was located on the eastern shore of Lake Calhoun where Saint Mary's Greek Orthodox Church now stands. This drawing of the cabin was based on the detailed descriptions later given by the Pond brothers. Gideon Pond described the cabin of "oak logs, carefully peeled," as 12 feet wide by 16 feet long, with tamarack logs from a local grove holding up the roof. The cabin had one window, a gift of Major Lawrence Taliaferno, and a door with a lock. The cost of the cabin was one shilling, used for nails. Gideon Pond also recalled the early days of the cabin: "the 'formal opening' exercises consisted in reading of a section from the old book by the name of the Bible, and prayer to Him who was its acknowledged author. The 'banquet' consisted of mussels from the lake, flour, and water." The site of the cabin itself had been selected by Cloudman. As Gideon Pond recalled, "the reason he gave for the selection was that 'from that point the loons would be visible on the lake.'" The Ponds lived in the cabin until 1836. The cabin was torn down in 1839 and its materials used for fortifications during the ongoing Dakota-Chippewa conflicts. (Courtesy Minneapolis Public Library.)

Colonel William King's Lake Calhoun Pavilion was built in 1877 at the bluff above what is now 35th Street and East Lake Calhoun Boulevard. King, one of the founders of the *Minneapolis Tribune*, owned large tracts of land in south Minneapolis and the Uptown area. The pavilion was later purchased by real estate magnate L.F. Menage and was turned into a hotel named the Lyndale. In addition to the attractions offered by the lake itself, visitors to the hotel could enjoy the dancing hall, billiards, and a wide variety of other pursuits. The fashionable resort hotel was destroyed by fire in 1888. (Courtesy Minneapolis Public Library.)

The four-story Lake Calhoun pavilion featured 14-foot-high verandas on the second and third floors with unencumbered views of the lake. "Its two broad verandas look down so invitingly upon the water that one naturally resolves to test their utility as soon as the trip around the lake is over," wrote the author of one tourist brochure. The pavilion's grand ballroom was the site of many of the Twin Cities' most elaborate social events of the 1870s and 1880s. Guests arrived at the pavilion via a train that ran from downtown Minneapolis to 34th Street. (Courtesy Minneapolis Public Library.)

Visitors to Lake Calhoun's resort hotels during the late 1870s enjoyed trips around the lake on a double-decker, side-wheeled steamer named *Hattie*. *Hattie* was owned and operated by the Lyndale and Minnetonka Motor Line. An 1879 tourist guide informed visitors that "a cozy little steamboat has been fitted up, at a considerable expense, which will meet all trains from the city. The new steamer can carry comfortably 350 passengers, and could carry 400 if necessary. It is a very neat and pretty little boat, being just what has been needed on Calhoun for many years." *Hattie* ceased operation in 1881 due to Lake Calhoun's increased competition

with Lake Minnetonka. The boat has not survived; at the end of her service she was towed to the center of the lake and burned. (Courtesy Minneapolis Public Library.)

The Lyndale Street Railway brought city residents and tourists to the shores of Lake Calhoun during the late 1870s and 1880s. The Minneapolis, Lyndale and Lake Calhoun Railway was headed by Colonel William McCrory, who received permission from the city in 1879 to run steam trains in Minneapolis. The trains carried approximately 60 passengers and ran every 45 minutes. In 1879, the year the railway opened, round-trip tickets cost 25¢ and a round-trip ticket including a ride on the company-owned lake steamer *Hattie* cost 35¢. Local residents or long-term visitors could purchase monthly passes for $3. Unfortunately for the Lake Calhoun business owners, the lake's resort hotels soon faced stiff competition from Lake Minnetonka. The train line was extended to Minnetonka in 1881, and the name was changed to the Minneapolis, Lyndale and Minnetonka Railway. (Courtesy Hennepin History Museum.)

Around the turn of the century, the area surrounding Lake Calhoun still contained parcels of undeveloped land. This group of University of Minnesota law students spent the summer of 1901 at a Lake Calhoun campsite. In their case, camping did not mean going without luxury. (Courtesy Hennepin History Museum.)

Early lake paths such as this one would later be expanded into a complex system of paved boulevards, walking paths, and bicycle paths. (Courtesy Minneapolis Public Library.)

Ice harvesting companies were formed on the banks of Lake Calhoun as early as the 1880s. The Boston Ice Company and the Cedar Lake Ice Company both had buildings on the north shore of the lake. The ice houses were located near the railroad tracks, and thus could provide ice for both local businesses and homes as well as for destinations requiring rail travel. Although the ice companies provided essential services for the city, not all residents approved of them. Local residents complained in 1899 that they feared that the companies were taking ice from the lake in such large quantities that the lake's water level would drop. The ice houses were demolished in 1909 after the Park Board finished acquiring the land surrounding Lake Calhoun. "The removal of the dilapidated and unsightly ice houses from the north shore of the Lake in 1909," wrote Theodore Wirth, "was welcomed by the entire city." Although the ice buildings were demolished, the ice companies themselves continued to operate, and older Uptown residents may recall hitching rides on the ice sleds that delivered ice to homes and businesses throughout the city. (Courtesy Minneapolis Public Library.)

The east side of Lake Calhoun was acquired by the Park Board in 1885. The area was briefly known as "Calhoun Terrace" and included a street named Calhoun Avenue. The street was extended south in 1887. During this time the street was graded and landscaped, becoming the early version of Calhoun Boulevard. By 1909 the land around the lake's shore, including the ice houses and barns, had been purchased, and the Park Board set to work implementing their plans. Both the Boulevard and the streetcar tracks connecting Uptown with distant areas of the city and suburbs are visible in this photograph. (Courtesy Hennepin History Museum.)

Nineteenth-century Minneapolis residents would hardly recognize Lake of the Isles today. The lake, once surrounded by swamps, originally had four islands. Subsequent dredging projects done by the Park Board reduced the number of islands to two. The modern shape of Lake of the Isles dates from 1911, when the Park Board completed a massive dredging project. During the period from 1907 to 1911, more than one-half million cubic yards of fill, primarily silt and peat, were removed from the shallow lake and surrounding wetlands. The lake's surviving islands were enlarged at this time. At the completion of the project, Lake of the Isles had been transformed from a lake and swamp consisting of 100 acres of water and 33 acres of dry land to a lake and park area with 120 acres of water and 80 acres of dry land. (Courtesy Minneapolis Public Library.)

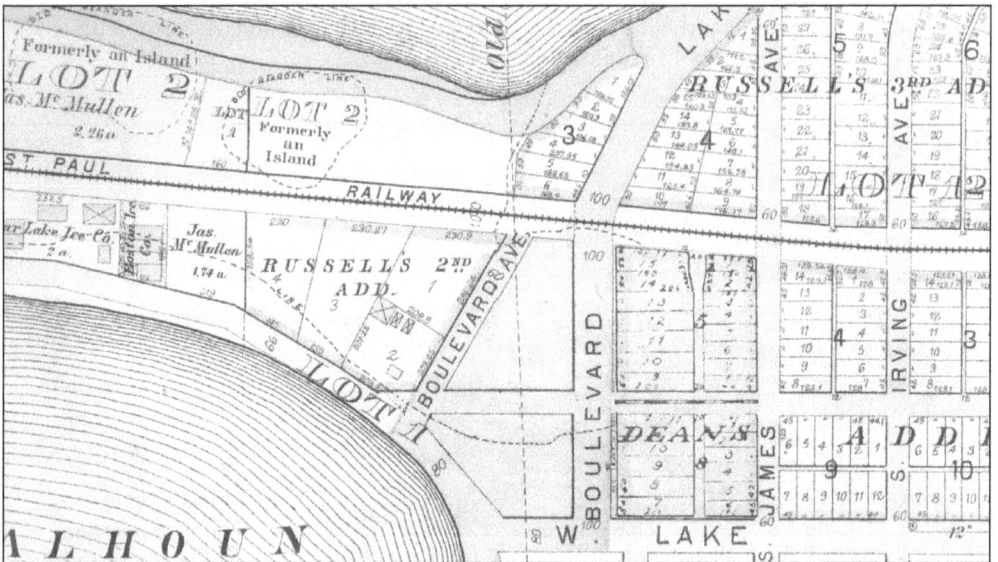

This 1890 map demonstrates the dramatic changes that took place in the area now known as Uptown during the late 1880s and early 1890s. The land between Lake of the Isles and Lake Calhoun had been divided into small lots, and the shape of Lake of the Isles had begun to change through dredging projects. This map shows the location of Lake of the Isles' former islands. Notice also that the map shows the ice houses on the north shore of Lake Calhoun. (Courtesy Hennepin History Museum.)

16

The building of the Chicago, Milwaukee and Saint Paul Railway line through Uptown in 1884 led to early dredging and filling, as dry land was created for the train tracks. Several years later, Lake of the Isles became the first Minneapolis lake to be dredged by the Park Board. Dredging machines such as this one removed large quantities of fill from Lake of the Isles and its swamps. The end result of multiple dredging projects spanning several decades was a distinct shoreline, the removal of two islands, the removal of swamp areas, and the creation of walking paths and a driving road on previously unusable land. (Courtesy Minneapolis Public Library.)

Dredging at Lake Calhoun occurred in two phases, the first one during the years 1911–1915, and the second one from 1923–1925. During the first stage, the beaches at Lake Street, Upton Avenue, and 33rd Street were created on man-made land. During the second stage, paved roads circling the lakes were created for the now-popular automobile. Much of the lake was originally surrounded by wetlands; these were eliminated by the conclusion of the dredging project. In recent years people have come to better appreciate the environmental value of wetlands, and there has been a movement to restore some wetlands to the lake. (Courtesy Hennepin History Museum.)

On July 5, 1911, Minneapolis residents gathered to celebrate the linking of Lake Calhoun and Lake of the Isles by canal. The two lakes were at the same height, and it was possible to create a channel connecting the two. The primary difficulties were from the large number of bridges that would be necessary to carry both carriage and railroad traffic over such a channel. More than six bridges were constructed, with the costs covered by the Park Board and the railroad companies. During the week of July 2–8, 1911, the city celebrated the linking of the lakes with a grand celebration. The official linking of the lakes was celebrated with special speeches and ceremonies, and the sailing of the *Maid of the Isles* under the bridges from one lake to the other. (Courtesy Minneapolis Public Library.)

The water between Lakes Calhoun and Isles, known as the lagoon, was initially dredged for the purpose of creating dry land bridge approaches and a higher street level. The designs for the six bridges over the lagoon were selected through a design contest. Twenty-five entries were submitted by applicants from around the nation. This winning bridge, pictured, was designed by William Pierce Cowles and Cecil Bayless Chapman of Minneapolis. The concrete bridge with limestone facing was completed in 1911. (Courtesy Minneapolis Public Library.)

Two

PARKS AND RECREATION

Uptown's lakes and parks have always offered residents many different options for outdoor recreation. During nice summer days, Lake Calhoun's waters have historically filled with sailboats and its beaches with swimmers. Lake of the Isles' walking paths have long been a favorite destination for evening rambles. The lagoon, the waters connecting Lake Calhoun with Lake of the Isles, has been a much-loved canoeing destination since it opened in 1911. Bicyclists have flocked to both lakes since the late nineteenth century. Today, rollerbladers share these bike paths. Uptown's stables, historically concentrated along 29th Street, provided homes for the horses that traveled Lake of the Isles' bridle path during the 1930s and 1940s.

The wintertime offered different lake-related attractions. The cleared skating rink on Lake of the Isles offered wintertime fun for residents of all ages. Fishermen fished year-round, bringing ice houses onto the frozen surface of Lake Calhoun. Ice boats, sleigh rides, and riding competitions have all been a part of Uptown's wintertime lake history.

Uptown offers other outdoor recreation possibilities beyond those offered by Lakes Calhoun and Isles. Bryant Square, located at 31st and Bryant, had a warming house and skating rink of its own, as well as a playground, tennis courts, and baseball fields. Mueller Park is a more recent addition, and was opened in the 1970s.

Fifteen young men came together in the summer of 1877 to form the Lurline Rowing Club on the shores of Lake Calhoun. The club quickly became the most prestigious rowing club in the Twin Cities, with members paying a $10 annual membership fee supplemented by a $1 monthly usage fee. In 1887 the Park Board acquired the land surrounding the eastern shores of Lake Calhoun. Although the Park Board required that most businesses in the area leave the land, they agreed to allow the Lurline Rowing Club to build a boat house "worthy of the club." A stipulation of the agreement was that the club would not engage in commercial transactions such as the selling or renting of boats. The club maintained a boat house at Lake Street and Lake Calhoun Boulevard. (Courtesy Minneapolis Public Library.)

The Lurline Rowing Club's regattas once attracted as many as 5,000 spectators to the shores of Lake Calhoun. "Its annual regattas are among the most popular social occasions," wrote Isaac Atwater in 1893. Invitations such as this one, issued in 1886, welcomed special guests to the festivities. (Courtesy Hennepin History Museum.)

On the back of this photograph someone has written "a speed sleigh but *not* a speedy team." The man and his horse posed for this photograph on Lake of the Isles during the winter of 1905–1906. (Courtesy Hennepin History Museum.)

The City of Minneapolis has a long history of stocking its lakes with fish, beginning as early as 1890. Park Board records from 1911 list 500,000 pike perch, 7,000,000 walleye, and 5,000 young crappies released into Lake Calhoun Although unproven, many also believed that Atlantic salmon had somehow made their way into the lake. (Courtesy Minneapolis Public Library.)

The Park Board approached a variety of sources for assistance in stocking the city's lakes with fish, and received help from the federal government, the State Game and Fish Commission, and the Isaac Walton League. Local fishermen enjoyed fishing from the sides of the lakes as well as from the numerous boats available for hire on Lake Calhoun during most of the twentieth century. Fishermen in the 1930s, for example, could rent one of 15 rowboats from the Lake Calhoun refectory for the cost of $1 per day. (Courtesy Minneapolis Public Library.)

The city's first bathhouse at Lake Calhoun was constructed in 1890, and initially served only men. After angry protests from women, the city relented and built the women a bathhouse of their own. The elaborate bathhouse shown here, located on the north shore of the lake, opened in 1912. The building cost more than $40,000 to construct, and could accommodate more than 1,200 people at one time. In addition to the bathhouse, other improvements made at the same time included the dredging of a new swimming beach. Visitors to Lake Calhoun traveled to the beach in their regular clothing and used the bathhouse to change into their bathing gear. In the early years, the city placed restrictions on appropriate attire, mandating that women's bloomers must reach six inches below the knees. (Courtesy Hennepin History Museum.)

The 1912 bathhouse was built without roofs in the dressing rooms. This was not a problem when the bathhouse was first built, but when the Calhoun Beach Club was erected across the street, its residents had a clear view into the bathhouse's interior. The bathhouse was replaced by a modern structure in 1950, this one with a roof. (Courtesy Minneapolis Public Library.)

This photo, taken in the mid-1930s by area resident Clarence Nelson, shows Lake Calhoun's main beach. A line of outer ropes marked the beginning of deep waters; approximately 15 feet beyond the ropes was a low resting dock. Also shown in this photograph are a low lifeguard tower and a diving tower with spring boards at both the 10-foot and the 25-foot level. A lifeguard patrols the beach in a rowboat. (Courtesy Clarence Nelson.)

Howard "Junior" Emerson is shown leaping from the water during the summer of 1936. Swimming was just one of many popular summer pastimes for neighborhood boys during the 1930s. Another activity was exploring the many closed-up commercial buildings that dotted the area during the Depression years. The Calhoun Beach Club building, visible beyond the beach, had been abandoned and boarded up in 1929. Neighborhood boys occasionally pried boards off the windows and doors and explored the empty interior. "Quite a few other closed-down buildings, including one on the corner of Lake Street and East Lake Calhoun Boulevard," recalls former area resident Clarence Nelson, "beckoned adventurous young explorers." (Courtesy Clarence Nelson.)

"A fully equipped bath house at which suits, towels, and lockers can be rented is located on the west side of the lake near Dean Boulevard," wrote a visitor to the lake in 1936. "There is also a refectory in the building." (Courtesy Hennepin History Museum.)

Clarence Nelson describes this Lake Calhoun photograph, taken in September of 1941, as "a boyhood attempt at 'art photography' on the cheap. I taped one glass from a pair of yellow sunglasses over a Baby Brownie camera lens to try for darker sky effects with the black and white film of that day." He took the photo while standing at the Lake Street Refectory. (Courtesy Clarence Nelson.)

Stables, interspersed with industrial development, lined 29th Street. The Park Riding Academy was located at 29th and Emerson. In 1940, Park Board Director of Education Karl Raymond formed a Park Board Riding Club based at the stable to encourage horseback riding among Minneapolis residents. Members could ride Jug, Pepper, Vanilla, Cricket, Blue, Pal, or Adobe during one of the seven different equestrian classes offered. It's not surprising that this photograph shows only women; all but 11 out of the 151 initial members were female. (Courtesy Minneapolis Public Library.)

Riding was a popular Uptown pastime during the 1930s and 1940s. "Extensive use of the bridle paths around Lake of the Isles, Calhoun, and Cedar Lakes, and in Kenwood and Glenwood Parks, indicates that horseback riding is becoming more popular in the city this year," reported the *Lake District Advocate* in 1930. The bridle path ringing Lake of the Isles was graveled during the 1924–1925 Park Board construction season, along with other improvements to the roads. (Courtesy Minneapolis Public Library.)

26

Mrs. Bradshaw of the Minneapolis Junior League took these Girl Scouts on a bicycle ride around Lake of the Isles in 1947. Bicycling around the lakes has been a popular activity with Uptown residents ever since the late nineteenth century. (Courtesy Minneapolis Public Library.)

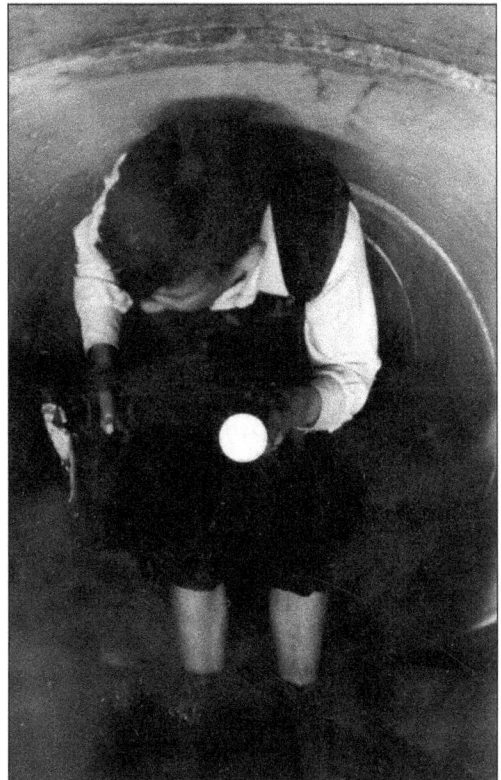

The Uptown area offered many interesting adventures for children growing up in the 1930s. Maurice "Shorty" Delong is shown here in a storm sewer tunnel that flowed into Lake Calhoun at 36th Street and East Lake Calhoun Boulevard. Rumor had it that the pipes were part of a larger system, in which an adventurous explorer could find his or her way from Lake Calhoun to the lake in Lakewood Cemetery to Lake Harriet and eventually to Minnehaha Falls. The storm sewers offered plenty of entertainment possibilities; Shorty is carrying a bullhead that he speared during his time in the sewer. (Courtesy Clarence Nelson.)

The Park Board acquired the land for Bryant Square Park, located at Bryant Avenue and 31st Street, in 1904. The land was to be used for what was then called the Eighth Ward Park. The park was set in a depression, or "hole," with concrete stairs at each corner leading down into the park itself. The steep banks offered protection from strong winds to those within. The hill to the north of the park building was used for tobogganing during the winter. During the summer there were three tennis courts in the south side of the park (not shown). The park was graded in the early 1970s, creating the modern profile with only a small depression on the southern side remaining. Visible behind the park is the Lyndale Congregational Church, now the Lyndale United Church of Christ. (Courtesy Minneapolis Park Board.)

Clarence "Junior" Nelson, Anna Nelson, and Russell Nelson are shown here in 1932 or 1933 sitting on a bench in Bryant Square. Behind them, the hill at the north side of the park is visible; this was the sledding hill used by neighborhood children during the winter. The Nelson family lived two blocks from the park during the 1930s and 1940s, and Clarence Nelson Jr. recalls spending every day here during the winter, regardless of the temperature. In the summer, local children congregated at the park to use the playground and play football in the grassy areas. This photograph was taken by Clarence Nelson Sr. (Courtesy Clarence Nelson.)

The warming house, located in the middle of the park, served Bryant Square's skaters during the winter months. A wooden walkway with a railing led from the warming house to the skating rink in the southern portion of the park. Skaters played games such as "pum-pum-pullaway" and prisoners' base tag. The skating rink had some outdoor lighting, essential for a city in which the sun set early during the winter months. Many of the skaters at Bryant Square, young and old alike, had likely attended an Ice Follies production or a Minneapolis Millers hockey game at the indoor Minneapolis Arena, located several blocks away. The original stucco warming building was replaced with a modern park building in 1971. (Courtesy Hennepin History Museum.)

The Mall, a 4.57-acre piece of landscaped grassy areas and walking paths stretching along the Milwaukee and Saint Paul Railway Company's train tracks between Hennepin and Lake Calhoun Boulevard, was created by the Park Board in 1912. (Courtesy Minneapolis Park Board.)

Mueller Park, located at 25th and Bryant, was officially dedicated on November 2, 1977. Homes on the future park's lot were purchased by the Park Board and demolished to make room for the two-acre park. The construction of the park was a victory for the neighborhood, as it was initially opposed by the Minneapolis Park Board. It was named for beloved neighborhood activists Bob and Herb Mueller. Shown here are, from left to right: unknown, Herb Mueller, Park Board President Gilbert, Bob Mueller, Alderman Munnich, Governor Rudy Perpich, and an unidentified woman. (Courtesy Minneapolis Park Board.)

Three

THE NEIGHBORHOODS

Minneapolis is a city of neighborhoods. Most of these neighborhoods have formally defined names and boundaries. These boundaries are by nature artificial, and do not always reflect the realities of neighborhood life. Uptown is a large community made up of smaller neighborhoods. Hennepin Avenue and Lake Street, Uptown's two main arteries, divide the area into four quadrants. These neighborhoods, officially named CARAG, ECCO, Lowry Hill East (the Wedge), and East Isles, all share a larger Uptown identity.

Uptown's neighborhoods have developed in different stages. The area initially consisted of large tracts of land used primarily for agriculture. By the 1890s these large land parcels had begun to be divided in earnest, and the grid streets familiar today were laid out. Some of the land was too swampy or sandy for home construction. These areas were later filled in and developed as the neighborhoods grew in density. During the 1920s, a large number of duplexes and apartment houses were built in the area, more so than in any other area of the city. Today turn-of-the-century homes, 1920s houses and duplexes, grand apartment buildings, and modern homes and apartments share the same blocks and neighborhoods. New development persists, and Uptown continues to adapt to the changing times and needs of the city.

Small stores and gas stations have always been common sights throughout the residential areas. Many of these commercial nodes still exist, and still provide a quick place for residents to pick up a gallon of milk or a pint of ice cream. During the 1990s, a number of these local commercial spaces were converted into coffee houses, a trend that appears to have permanently altered Uptown's neighborhoods. These popular coffee houses, most of them locally owned and operated, are today's community gathering places.

31

In 1851, Roswell Russell of Saint Anthony purchased a large piece of land encompassing the area between Lake of the Isles and Lyndale Avenue, and from what is now 26th Street to Lake Street. The Russell family moved from their home in Saint Anthony to a new mansard-roofed brick mansion in 1873. Their home was located near what is now the intersection of Hennepin and 28th Street. After the house was demolished around 1900, the corner stood empty until 1907, when West High School was built in its place. (Courtesy Hennepin History Museum.)

Roswell P. Russell was one of Minneapolis's early settlers. In 1847 Russell opened a store in Saint Anthony, believed to have been the first store in what was to become Minneapolis. Russell married Marion Patch in 1848. Pictured here is the Russell family in the mid-1880s. (Courtesy Hennepin History Museum.)

The Russell farm was located in what were the outskirts of the city during the 1880s. The cows in this Uptown-area pasture are a reminder of the area's early agricultural heritage. Within a decade of when this mid-1880s photograph was taken, the landscape of the area had already started to change significantly. "This land, for many years only valuable for its agricultural uses," wrote Isaac Atwater of Russell's land in 1893, "has been laid out into blocks and lots, to accommodate the expanding population, and has been, more than the various lines of business which he [Russell] has undertaken and pursued with such industry, the chief source of his comfortable financial situation." (Courtesy Hennepin History Museum.)

Two of the Russell children posed with their horses for this photograph taken during the mid-1880s. One of the horses was named Thor. (Courtesy Hennepin History Museum.)

Lemuel Peppard, his wife Jettie Peppard, and their son, Thomas, posed with their horse, Maud, outside of their home at 23rd and Bryant during a turn-of-the-century winter. The house was completed in 1900, and this photograph was possibly taken to commemorate their new home. (Courtesy Hennepin History Museum.)

Minneapolis's streetcar system had been first proposed in 1873. Although the first line was a failure, one investor, Colonel William King, and a young lawyer named Thomas Lowry reorganized the Minneapolis Street Railway Company in 1875. Lowry had become interested in real estate and believed that a better transportation system would allow more people to access homes farther from the city's core, thereby increasing the value of his real estate ventures. Lowry was right, and the development of an extensive railway system allowed the city to grow. This streetcar from the Hennepin, Lyndale, and Lake line was photographed outside the streetcar company's horse barns on Dupont and 28th Street in 1885. These barns, called the Lyndale Barns, were built in 1884 and were used to house horses through 1890. The Uptown area was still predominantly home to farms and resorts in the mid-1880s, when this photograph was taken, but the development of the railway system not only meant better access to the lakes for day-trippers, but also allowed an increasing number of people to live in the area year-round. (Courtesy Minneapolis Public Library.)

34

This 1889 Queen Anne-style house, located at 3501 Bryant, was built in 1889 by William K. Chapman for $5,000. In addition to the house, the property also contained a barn at the southeast corner. The house was among the first built along Bryant Avenue. It was built with indoor plumbing, although electricity was not installed until 1931. It has undergone many architectural changes over the course of its history, including the removal of the porte cochere, upper porch roof, and railing. Prudence Maria MacKenzie purchased the house in 1901 and lived there with her parents and siblings. Members of the MacKenzie family continued to live in the house until 1986. This photo possibly shows Prudence's mother, Eliza Ann MacKenzie, c. 1910. The current owner has conducted extensive historical research and is in the process of restoring the house to its earlier appearance. (Courtesy Joseph Metzler.)

The 20-room Forman Mansion, located at 3450 Irving Avenue, was built in 1901 on the foundations of the former Lyndale Hotel. Mr. Forman died in 1912, leaving Mrs. Forman alone in the house until her death in 1949. She was much-loved in the neighborhood, and was known for her kindness as well as for her eccentricity, her "outlandish clothes," and her entertaining dinner parties. "She was the grandest woman I ever knew," declared one acquaintance. She allowed area children to visit the mansion and to play on its grounds. After Mrs. Forman's death, the property was purchased by the Northwestern National Life Insurance Company with the intention of using the site for an office building. Many were sad to see the grand mansion demolished, but times were changing and most people were unable to maintain such large homes. "It's too bad that it has to be torn down," said one former visitor to the mansion, "but no one wants it. Six maids couldn't take care of it." Although local residents accepted that the mansion was to be demolished, there was significant neighborhood opposition to the company's plans. The idea of an office building was ultimately abandoned. Instead, Saint Mary's Greek Orthodox Church built a church on the property in 1955. The church has since become an integral part of the neighborhood. (Courtesy Minneapolis Public Library.)

The Gates Mansion, located at 2501 East Lake of the Isles Boulevard, was completed in 1914. The record-setting house—its $1 million construction costs made it the most expensive house ever built in Minnesota and its expansive floor plan made it the largest house ever built in Minneapolis—was to be the home of multi-millionaire Charles Gates, son of John "Bet-a-Million" Gates. The four-story, 38,000-square-foot house and its gardens took up nearly one entire city block. The house was designed by Chicago architects Marshall and Fox. (Courtesy Hennepin History Museum.)

After Charles Gates of Illinois married Minneapolis native Florence Hopwood, the couple made plans to return to her hometown. Gates had the mansion built to serve as their new home and informed local journalists that he was building his wife a "cottage on the lake." The house was to be built with 40 bedrooms, gold doorknobs, parquet floors, crystal chandeliers, tennis courts, a ballroom, and a large pipe organ. The most significant aspect of the new house was its air conditioning system. The Gates Mansion became the first house in the United States to be air conditioned. Gates was definitely ahead of his time—most retail stores did not get air conditioning until the mid-1920s, and the White House did not get air conditioning until 1930. The system took up an entire room in the basement of the mansion, and cooled the space through an elaborate system of fans and water. The unit was seven feet high, six feet wide, and 20 feet long. (Courtesy Hennepin History Museum.)

Gates and his bride were never to enjoy life in their elaborate "cottage on the lake." Before the house was completed, Gates developed appendicitis. Following an appendectomy, he attempted a hunting trip to Wyoming with "Buffalo Bill" Cody. While there, he fell ill again, this time with fatal results. Mrs. Gates remarried in 1916 and moved to the east coast. She sold the house to Dr. Dwight Brooks of Saint Paul in 1923. Brooks never lived in the house, although he did allow non-profits to use the home for fundraising activities. Following his death in 1929, the family was unable to sell the large house. It was demolished in 1933. (Courtesy Hennepin History Museum.)

The land shown here, located at 26th and Irving, was originally part of Roswell Russell's 1850 land purchase. The majority of these houses were built in the first decade of the twentieth century, a time when the area was changing from predominantly farmland and summer resorts to a year-round city neighborhood. (Courtesy Hennepin History Museum.)

In 1883 Professor H.W.S. Cleveland of Chicago presented the city with a report entitled "Suggestions for a System of Parks and Parkways for the City of Minneapolis." His report laid out suggestions for creating an attractive city filled with wide, tree-lined boulevards that would have the added benefit of serving as barriers to urban fires. Hennepin Avenue, between its intersection with Lyndale and its end at Lakewood Cemetery at 36th Street, was suggested as one of these boulevards. In 1884 the city accordingly decided to widen Hennepin Avenue by 22 feet. As an official boulevard, commercial activities were restricted until 1905, when the Park Board voted to ease restrictions and end Hennepin Avenue's days as a boulevard. Businesses quickly moved in, and earlier homes, such as the house shown here on the left (at 26th and Hennepin), mingled side by side with new commercial buildings housing grocers, cleaners, hardware stores, and other neighborhood necessities. (Courtesy Hennepin History Museum.)

This photograph, taken in 1923, shows construction at the corner of Emerson and 34th Street. The photographer was standing at 3412 Emerson, looking north. Many, although not all, of the homes on the 3300 block of Emerson, visible on the other side of the intersection, were completed in 1922. (Courtesy Hennepin History Museum.)

This rooftop view from West High School, likely taken sometime in the 1920s, shows the relatively new development on the former Russell lands. (Courtesy Minneapolis Public Schools.)

The view of the rears of these apartments, located near 26th and Emerson, is shown as seen from neighboring Jefferson Junior High during the 1920s. Although some of the apartment buildings on the block still stand, others have since been demolished to create room for a school parking lot. (Courtesy Minneapolis Public Schools.)

This West Lake Street home, built in 1909, was one of many sold by the Confer Brothers Realty Company of Minneapolis. Their slogan, "Confer with Confer," was a familiar sight in the neighborhood for many years. The sign in front of this home advertises a "modern duplex and cottage in rear," to be sold at a "snap price." (Courtesy Hennepin History Museum.)

40

This house on a relatively quiet block of Hennepin Avenue was built in 1919. (Courtesy Hennepin History Museum.)

This photograph of the rear of a home on 28th and Irving can be found in the extensive historical Confer Brothers real estate files at the Hennepin History Museum. (Courtesy Hennepin History Museum.)

This indoor-outdoor porch belongs to a local house built in 1908. Like so many houses in Uptown, the home was built on the former Russell property. (Courtesy Hennepin History Museum.)

The elaborate interior of this 1900 house on Irving Avenue was likely photographed when it was put up for sale by its owners. Many local homes still retain original woodwork and lighting fixtures such as the ones shown here. (Courtesy Hennepin History Museum.)

The Lindskoog florist shop occupied this building on the corner of 28th and Emerson during the 1970s. Ed and Myrt Peterson built the structure in the 1940s to house their floral shop, the Edward Peterson Florist Shop. It featured beautiful slate floors, Art Deco light fixtures, a goldfish pond, and a greenhouse. Lindskoog moved into the building in 1968 and remained until 1979, when the business moved to a new downtown location. (Courtesy Ray Harris.)

The Granada Apartment Building was built in 1929. Its Lagoon Avenue location gave its residents convenient access to the Uptown business core. The building is one of many neighborhood apartment buildings heavily inspired by Moorish design. Like many apartment buildings of its size, the Granada also had a small retail space in the basement. Among other businesses to occupy the space was Trudi's Beauty Shop. (Courtesy Warner Properties.)

Uptown's portion of Hennepin Avenue became known as the city's premier apartment house street by the 1920s. Apartment buildings in a range of sizes offered residents diverse housing options. This building at 27th and Hennepin was built in 1909, four years after Hennepin Avenue ceased to officially exist as a boulevard. The building still stands today, although the second-story porch has been enclosed. (Courtesy Hennepin History Museum.)

In 1923 the *Lake District Advocate* commented on the connection between apartment buildings and the rapid growth of Uptown's business core: "The marked prosperity of this corner [Hennepin and Lake] is undoubtedly accounted for by its location and the tremendous growth of apartments in this district." The residents of this apartment house undoubtedly did their part to support local business. (Courtesy Warner Properties.)

Construction began on the nine-story Calhoun Beach Club in 1928. When the Depression struck in 1929, only the exterior had been completed. The shell of the building sat empty for the next 18 years. The building enjoyed a brief renaissance following World War II, and served as a popular Minneapolis nightspot. The club went bankrupt in 1954, at which point it was converted to a hotel with luxury apartments on the upper floors and a film studio on the second and third floors. In the 1960s the building underwent yet another change, and became a retirement home. In 1977 the building returned to its role as a social and athletic club. Today the building has been restored to its earlier grandeur, and once again houses luxury apartments overlooking Lake Calhoun. (Courtesy Hennepin History Museum.)

The businesses at the corner of 34th and Hennepin provided necessities of life for residents of the houses and apartments in the immediate area. Over the past century the corner has housed grocery stores, meat markets, florists, and, most recently, a coffee house. (Courtesy Michael Lander.)

45

These apartments at 28th and Dupont offered residents convenient access to transportation on Lake Street and Hennepin and Lyndale Avenues. The building was located a block away from the popular Minneapolis Arena. (Courtesy Warner Properties.)

This gas station on the southeast corner of 28th Street and Dupont became a Shell Petroleum fill station in 1930. It ceased business sometime in the 1950s. Gas stations, initially called fill stations, became a regular feature of the neighborhood during the late 1920s after the automobile became commonplace. (Courtesy Warner Properties.)

Four

COMMUNITY

Businesses and homes are not enough to create a community; libraries, churches, temples, fire stations, police stations, post offices, and the other assorted places are equally important for creating a sense of community. Uptown historically offered its residents all of the necessities of life. The area had its own police station, fire station, and post office, none of which exist today. Uptown's library, the Walker Branch Library, does still exist, although no longer in its original 1911 building.

For those looking for a spiritual community, Uptown offered a large number of churches and temples. Synagogues Adath Jeshurun and Temple Israel both called Uptown home, as did Joyce Methodist Church, Grace Presbyterian Church, Saint Mary's Greek Orthodox Church, the Third Church of Christ Scientist, and the Minnesota Zen Center. These organizations have often reached out to the larger community through their volunteer efforts and outreach programs.

Anchoring the southern end of Uptown and often the final stop for many Uptown residents is the Lakewood Cemetery. Lakewood was created as part of the rural cemetery movement and offered Minneapolis citizens a scenic burial setting perched between Lake Calhoun and Lake Harriet. For many years a thriving industry of cemetery-related businesses existed at Hennepin Avenue between 35th and 36th Streets, including a stone quarry, monument companies, and florists.

T.B. Walker donated the site for the original Walker Branch Library. At 29th and Hennepin, the library was conveniently located along a streetcar line. The $45,000 building was constructed in the Beaux Arts style and designed by Jerome Paul Jackson. The new library met the needs of the "well-to-do residents near Lake Calhoun and Lake of the Isles." This photograph, taken soon after the Walker Library opened in June of 1911, vividly demonstrates how the character of the Uptown business district has changed over time. The large trees, as well as the strip of grass separating sidewalk from street, serve as a reminder of the years in which Hennepin Avenue was designated a boulevard by the Minneapolis Park Board. (Courtesy Minneapolis Public Library.)

Branch libraries were conceived as a way to get books into the community and to provide more accessibility than could be offered by the main downtown library. The Minneapolis Public Library took its role in the community very seriously. Beginning in 1913, just two years after the Walker Branch Library was completed, branch librarians across the city completed surveys of their jurisdictions. They had instructions to study "the district, its people, their nationality, trades, and needs," and to "therefrom study the methods which the library can best use for the particular people served by each branch." (Courtesy Hennepin History Museum.)

This photograph, taken early in the library's history, shows three boys in the Walker Library's reference room. The library was a useful community resource for local students. (Courtesy Minneapolis Public Library.)

The former Walker Branch Library was located less than one block away from West High School. Shown here are students from West using the library's resources. The student standing and inspecting books with his back to the camera is wearing a West sweater. (Courtesy Minneapolis Public Library.)

This photograph, labeled "Story hour, a typical Saturday," shows some of the library's regular visitors. Branch libraries attempted to reach out to their local communities, and events such as story hour were and continue to be Walker Library staples. (Courtesy Minneapolis Public Library.)

The Walker Branch Library provided an ideal meeting space for clubs such as the Mushroom Club. This organization, one of the many clubs and organizations existing in the Uptown area, is shown inside the Walker Library in 1936. (Courtesy Minneapolis Public Library.)

A new Uptown library had first been proposed in 1967. The idea was discussed extensively before finally receiving approval in 1974. The approval was the first step in the long march towards a new library. Groundbreaking for the new Walker Library finally took place on June 22, 1979. (Courtesy Minneapolis Public Library.)

The new Walker Library was built on Hennepin across the street from the original library. The new structure was built underground with the hope that the underground construction would maximize available space and prove to be energy-efficient. The old library, visible across the street in this image, remained standing. It was placed on the National Register of Historic Places in 2000. (Courtesy Minneapolis Public Library.)

The new Walker Branch Library was completed and opened for business in 1981. The innovative design featured two lower levels with 18,500 square feet of space. A lower-level garden was visible through the lower-level windows, providing a sense of the outdoors as well as natural light. (Courtesy Minneapolis Public Library.)

As the Uptown area steadily moved away from resorts and agriculture to an outlying neighborhood of the city, complete with homes, apartments, and businesses, local residents began pressuring the city for a local fire station. The land at 35th and Hennepin was purchased by the city in 1903, and built Station 23 there in February of 1906. The new station was home to Engine 23 and Ladder 7. The rig shown in this 1939 photo is Ladder 5's 1932 Pirsch with the Minneapolis Fire Department's City Service Trailer #14. Former students of Calhoun Elementary School may remember visiting the station on school trips and being treated to the sound of sirens. (Courtesy Extra Alarm Association of the Twin Cities, Duane Troxel Memorial Library files.)

The brick two-story Station 23 was closed in 1946. The fire department had been offered an opportunity to build a station at the Naval Air base. To do so required the closing of an existing station, as there would otherwise not be enough firefighters to provide sufficient coverage for the new station. In 1991 the former fire station was converted into loft-style condominiums. (Courtesy Michael Lander.)

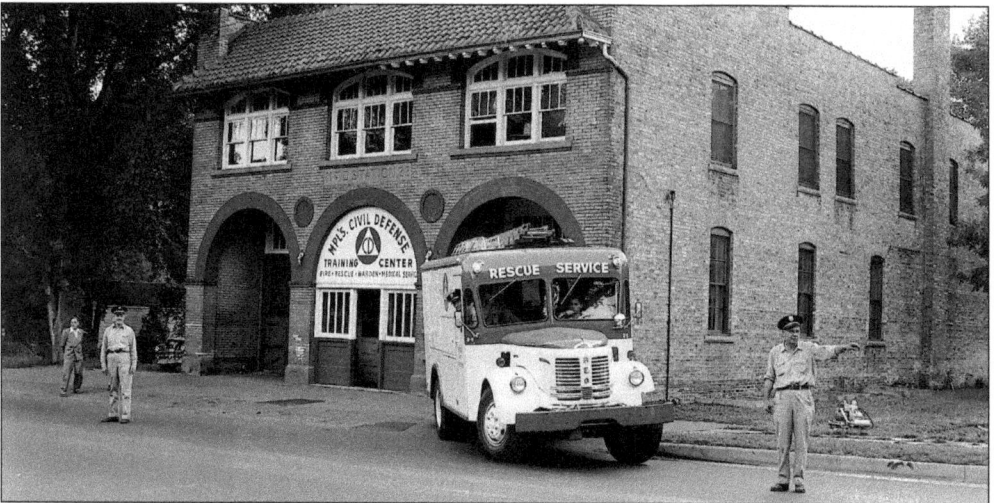

The former Minneapolis Fire Station 23 was turned into a Civil Defense Training Center following World War II. This 1954 photograph shows the center's large sign, advertising "Fire, Rescue, Warden, Medical Service." The Minneapolis Police Reserve operated under the umbrella of the Civil Defense in the 1950s through the late 1980s. The reservists received training in responding to emergencies, and practiced their crowd control skills at large community events such as the Aquatennial. (Courtesy Minnesota Historical Society.)

Minneapolis's Fifth Precinct Police Station was located at Bryant and Lake for many years. In 1930, the American Legion's Calhoun Post moved their headquarters to the community hall above the station; their 200 members organized an emergency relief troop at the station to assist the police department in case of an emergency. The building still stands, although the Police Department moved the precinct station to Nicollet Avenue in 1982. (Courtesy Minnesota Historical Society.)

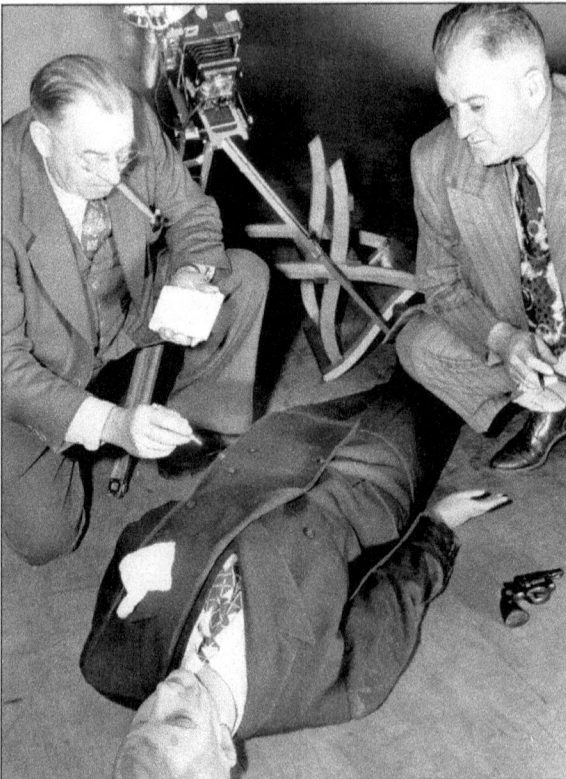

Shown here are Detective Supervisor Charles van Rickley and Detective Captain Clarence McLaskey. On the ground is Oscar, a dummy used for training purposes. Oscar was used by the FBI for a class conducted at the Bryant Avenue Police Station. (Courtesy Minneapolis Public Library.)

Lieutenant L.W. Mills, leader of the 1935 Lake Calhoun Memorial Day services, is shown here in front of the wheel and mast from the U.S.S. *Minnesota*. The wheel and mast were joined in 1930 by the bell from the U.S.S. *Minneapolis*. The U.S.S. *Minneapolis* was commissioned in 1894 and spent several years sailing on the United States' East Coast, the West Indies, northern Europe, and the Mediterranean. She was decommissioned in 1906 and spent the next decade in Philadelphia. She was put back in service for World War I, and spent much of the conflict escorting convoys in the North Atlantic. In March of 1921, she was decommissioned for the last time and sold for scrap metal. The U.S.S. *Minnesota* was commissioned in 1907. She served in northern Europe during World War I and was damaged by a German mine in 1918. She was decommissioned in 1921, and in 1924 the remains of the U.S.S. *Minnesota* were sold for scrap metal. (Courtesy Minneapolis Public Library.)

A combination boat house and refectory was built on Lake Calhoun in 1930 at a cost of more than $15,000. The one-story stucco building was also home to the Calhoun Yacht Club. More than 125 canoes were available for rental in 1936, at a cost of 30¢ an hour. The refectory was often used as the backdrop for Memorial Day commemorations, as was probably the case in this photograph. (Courtesy Hennepin History Museum.)

Lake Calhoun has often been a site for community events, including parades such as this one. (Courtesy Minneapolis Public Library.)

Welcome Ahepans!

Officers of the Philoptochos Society

Minneapolis, Minnesota

Seated, Left to Right: Mrs. Michael D. Boosalis, Mrs. George N. Boosalis, Rev. Gregory Carfopoulos, Mrs. James J. Dovolis and Mrs. Christ G. Pappas.

Standing, Left to Right: Mrs. Peter Vlassis, Mrs. Theodore, H. Pappas, Mrs. Christ Posis, Mrs. George Grammas and Mrs. Christ Legeros.

Greek Orthodox Ladies' Philoptochos Societies (Adelphotis) were developed under the Greek Orthodox Archdiocese of North and South America in 1931. This photo of a local branch was taken mid-1950s and features many members of the local Saint Mary's Greek Orthodox Church. (Courtesy Tian Barbatsis Dayton.)

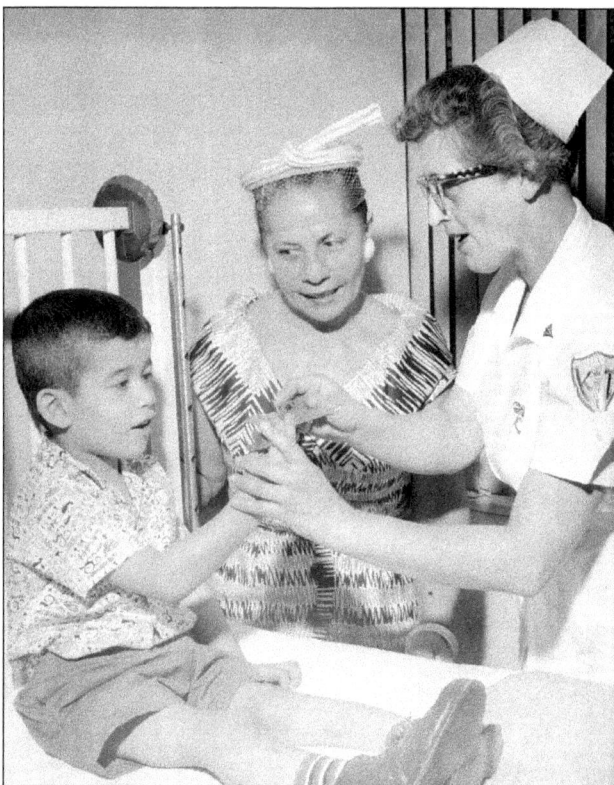

Uptown resident Anna Legeros is shown here translating between a young Greek boy and a Sister Kenny Institute nurse. The Sister Kenny Institute was world-famous for its treatment of polio. They called Saint Mary's Greek Orthodox Church when they required a volunteer Greek translator. Legeros, a member of Saint Mary's, assisted on many occasions. (Courtesy of Tian Barbatsis Dayton.)

This photograph was taken in 1936 and shows the second Third Church of Christ Scientist to be located in Uptown. The first building, dating to 1902, was located at Lake and Holmes. The new building was designed by local architecture firm Hewitt and Brown in 1919 and was completed in 1923. It was located on Lagoon Avenue. Due in part to the church's close proximity to the center of the Hennepin-Lake business district, there were often close ties between the business community and the Third Church of Christ Scientist. In 1930, for example, the church and the Uptown Business Association jointly built a large graveled parking lot "open to shoppers who visit the district." The congregation held its last service in the church in February of 1954 before moving to a new home in Linden Hills. (Courtesy Minneapolis Public Library.)

This image shows Grace Presbyterian Church, located on 28th Street and Humboldt. Grace was initially founded in 1884 in a home located at 34th and Garfield. The congregation moved to 28th Street in 1902. The building shown here dates from 1928. The church is now Grace Trinity Community Church. (Courtesy Hennepin History Museum.)

Adath Jeshurun was founded in 1884 and was the first conservative congregation of its kind west of Chicago. The Adath Jeshurun congregation moved to Uptown in 1927, after a member sold them the 34th and Dupont site for a good price. In April of 1927, more than 800 people attended a ceremony marking the laying of the new Dupont Avenue synagogue's cornerstone. Ceremonial trowels were given to attendees as souvenirs. In 1995, Adath Jeshurun moved to a new home in Minnetonka. The 34th and Dupont site is now home to the First Universalist Church of Minneapolis. (Courtesy Minneapolis Public Library.)

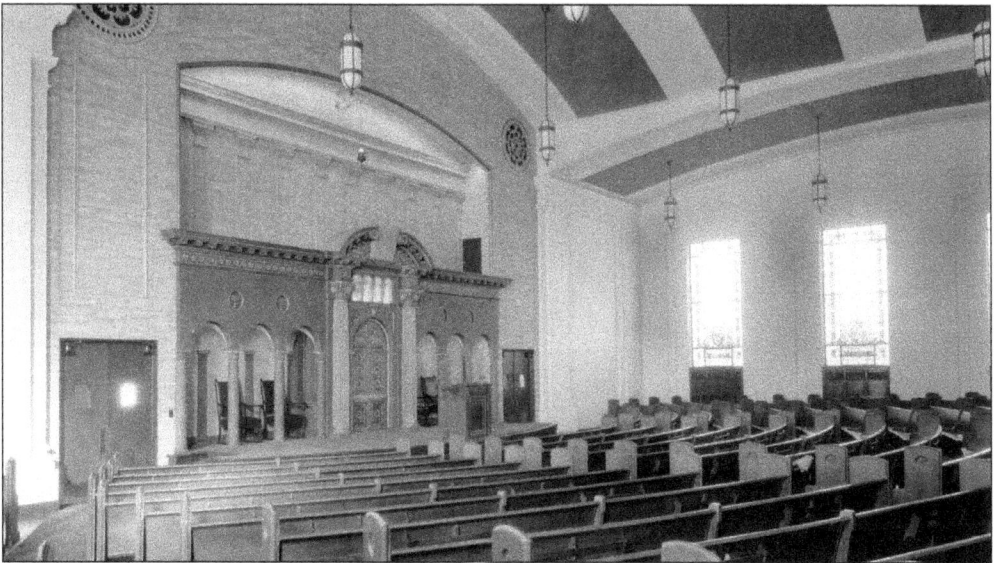

The new Adath Jeshurun synagogue was among the largest in the northwest when it was built. It seated 1,200 people, featured a theater and music hall for an additional 700 people, offered eight classrooms for 300 children, featured a dining hall, lockers and showers, a stage, a chapel, a balcony seating 200, a choir gallery, kitchen space, office space, and a study and library. The seats were leather upholstered opera chairs. This photo was taken in 1930. (Courtesy Minneapolis Public Library.)

The Joyce Methodist Church was originally founded as the Lake Street Methodist Episcopal Church in 1886. It was one of the first churches to serve the area and its growing population. Pastor James Teeter explained the reasoning behind the outreach efforts: "I am concerned with that district lying in the outskirts of the city, the territory to the East of Lakes Calhoun and Harriet and adjacent to Lake Street. There are little children, young people and adults living in this part of the city without church privileges." The church was initially located in the Town Hall at the corner of Lake Street and Fremont, a building that burned to the ground in 1895 and was rebuilt. In 1906, the church members shown here broke ground for a new building on the corner of 31st and Girard. It is believed that the Town Hall was moved to the new site from its Lake Street location and was incorporated into the new church complex. The growing congregation wanted to expand its space and move further away from the traffic of Lake Street. It was at this point that the church was renamed Joyce Memorial Methodist Episcopal Church in honor of Bishop Isaac Joyce. The new Spanish Mission-style building, complete with white stucco walls and red tile roof, still stands today. (Courtesy Joyce United Methodist Church.)

The Joyce choir of 1936 was led by Leif Ardressen. The impressive organ shown here was played by Miss Green. The organ was later destroyed by a devastating fire in 1943. The fire department responding to the fire believed that they could extinguish the fire quickly if allowed to smash the church's stained glass windows. The congregation wouldn't allow this to happen, and as a result much of the interior was destroyed. Despite the wartime economy, the church was restored. A new organ was purchased in 1946. (Courtesy Joyce United Methodist Church.)

Children have always been an important part of Joyce Church. Students from the Calhoun School, located across the street, often used the church's facilities. In 1966 Joyce established a nursery school to serve neighborhood children, and in 1969 the Joyce-Calhoun Child Care Center was created. Many children in the Uptown area were members of Joyce Church and attended Sunday school there weekly. An added bonus for Sunday school regulars was after-school access to the church's gymnasium. The children shown here were in Lola Hardy's Sunday school class. (Courtesy Joyce United Methodist Church.)

Joyce Church purchased the Dutton residence at 1222 West 31st Street in 1968. The home was renamed the Joyce House, and provided much-needed social services for area residents. In addition to a thrift store operating in the late 1960s, a food shelf was established under Pastor Doug Marx's tenure. The Emergency Food Shelf Program was created in 1969 and still operates today. (Courtesy Joyce United Methodist Church.)

The Smith residence was located at 24th and Emerson. In 1914, Temple Israel (then known by the name of Shaari Tov) member John Friedman offered to sell the house and its land to the Temple for $14,000. The deed included a stipulation that the site should be used for a future house of worship. The congregation accepted the offer, and the house was initially used for religious classes and meetings. The location was ideal for many of Temple Israel's members. Many of Minneapolis's Jewish residents were at that time living in what is now the Uptown area, and were within walking distance of the new site. The Smith House location was later used as the site for the new synagogue, built in 1928. (Courtesy Temple Israel.)

These young men and women were members of long-time Temple Israel Rabbi Minda's first confirmation class. They had all completed grade nine, and had reached at least age 15. Students in both the Pre-Confirmation and the Confirmation courses attended classes on both Saturday and Sunday mornings, as well as attended regular services. Once a month they took over the responsibility of running a service, giving the readings and conducting brief sermons. Rabbi Minda posed annually for an official class photo with his 20 to 25 students, this photograph being the first of what he would later refer to as his "rogues gallery"; the good-humored Minda later recounted that "it is not uncommon for someone to see my picture amongst the youngsters of the class of 1923 and innocently ask whether it is mine, and then again innocently remark—'you were good looking then.'" (Courtesy Temple Israel.)

Groundbreaking for Temple Israel, located on the former Smith residence site at 24th and Emerson, was held in the spring of 1927. The most architecturally significant element of the grand new Greek Revival structure was not its six two-story pillars facing Hennepin, nor its spacious interior, but instead, its revolutionary use of acoustic tiles. Temple member Jack Liebenberg used sugar beet stalks from northern Minnesota for the tiles. Liebenberg and partner Seeman Kaplan went on to great success as the upper Midwest's premier theater architects, due in large part to the early acoustic success of Temple Israel. (Courtesy Minneapolis Public Library.)

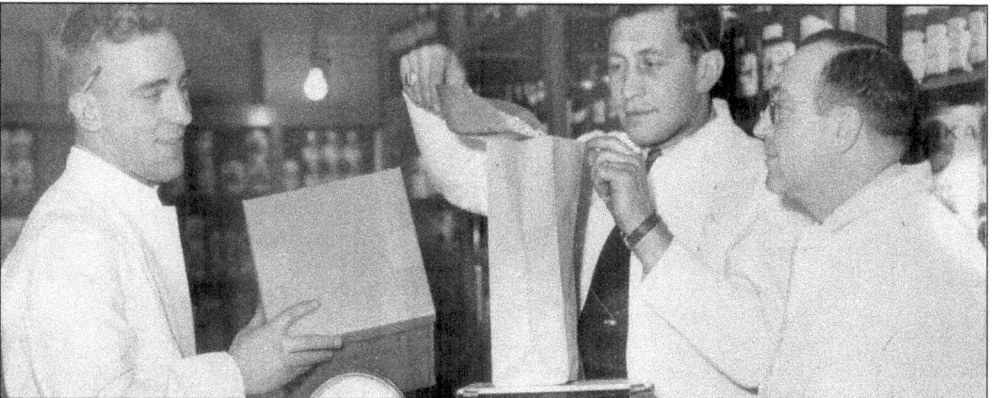

Like Adath Jeshurun, Uptown's other Jewish congregation, Temple Israel had financial difficulties during the Great Depression. The new synagogue had been financed based upon members' pledges. Many of these members found themselves unable to pay as promised. An annual carnival called "Rigadoo" was formed as a fundraiser. In just five years, Rigadoo generated $25,000, allowing Temple Israel to keep up its payments. Not everyone was happy with the need to resort to such fundraisers. Rabbi Minda described the following: "A canopy lighted by varied colored light bulbs reached from Emerson Avenue to the 24th Street side entrance of the temple. To see this, in front of our classic temple, almost broke my heart. There were also some of the aspects of the Rigadoo to which I had to close my eyes, with the feeling that these men and women conducting it were fighting for a principle involving honor and in keeping faith with our creditors." Despite his misgivings, the Rabbi did concede that "everyone, young and old, had a good time." These University of Minnesota football players are helping weigh groceries at the 1935 Rigadoo. (Courtesy Minneapolis Public Library.)

Rabbi Minda joined Temple Israel in 1921. The young rabbi oversaw a period of great growth in the congregation. In addition to all of his work within the congregation, he reached out to connect with the larger community. He was one of the founders of Minneapolis' Urban League and the Minneapolis Round Table of Christians and Jews. During Rabbi Minda's tenure, Temple Israel built their new home at 24th and Emerson. Minda helped found the Men's Club, helped create a Jewish art gallery and museum in the Temple, and oversaw the 1955 religious school addition to the building. He retired in 1963. This photograph was taken during Rosh Hashanah, 1947. (Courtesy Minneapolis Public Library.)

Temple Israel expanded once again in 1984. The congregation had become the tenth largest Reform congregation in North America, and additional space and amenities were needed to accommodate this growth. (Courtesy Temple Israel.)

Lakewood Cemetery anchors the far edge of Uptown and has been the final resting place for local residents since 1872. The cemetery was built as part of the national rural cemetery movement. Minneapolis residents wanted a cemetery in a beautiful location "out near the lake, where the encroachments of the city would never seriously interfere." The cemetery's founders purchased from William King a parcel of land on the rolling hills between Lake Calhoun and Lake Harriet, the one-time site of the Dakota village named Eatonville, and arguably one of the city's most beautiful locations. Lakewood Cemetery continued to expand, and by 1908 it consisted of 240 acres. Lakewood's rolling hills are covered with a broad range of monuments and tombstones. Those buried or commemorated here include important early Minneapolis families such as the Pillsburies, Washburns, and Walkers, more recent political heroes such as Hubert Humphrey and Paul Wellstone, and a memorial to the 18 men killed in one of Minneapolis's worst industrial disasters, the Washburn "A" Mill explosion of 1878. (Courtesy Hennepin History Museum.)

Lakewood's imposing red granite Romanesque gatehouse was built in 1889 at a cost of $35,000. The gatehouse, designed by Frank Read, provided the cemetery with a grand entrance as well as fireproof office space. (Courtesy Hennepin History Museum.)

Lakewood Cemetery was a popular late-nineteenth-century destination for day-trippers. It was not uncommon for visitors to the cemetery to bring a packed lunch and to spend all day wandering among the monuments and memorials. (Courtesy Hennepin History Museum.)

The mausoleum was a relatively modern addition to Lakewood Cemetery. Groundbreaking for the new building occurred in November of 1965, and the mausoleum was completed in 1967. The building offered space for 3,000 crypts and 2,000 niches. It was made of granite and steel, embellished with bronze and Italian marble, and decorated with crystal chandeliers and impressionist paintings. (Courtesy Hennepin History Museum.)

Five

SCHOOLS

Until the mid-1970s, it was possible for Uptown children to meet almost all of their educational needs locally. The local elementary school, Calhoun Elementary, opened in 1887. Its central Lake Street and Girard location put students in close proximity to the business district. The students frequently visited local institutions such as the fire station or the library, while the school in turn provided meeting space for many community organizations. Among others, the Hennepin-Lake Business Women's Association held their gym classes at the school during the 1930s. Calhoun Elementary School was closed and demolished in 1975 due in part to low enrollment.

After completing sixth grade at Calhoun, students moved north up Hennepin Avenue to Jefferson Junior High. There, they joined students from other nearby elementary schools, primarily Douglas and Lyndale Schools. Jefferson is still a school today, and is currently home to the Jefferson Community School's kindergarten through eighth-grade students.

In tenth grade, students moved to West High, located at 28th and Hennepin. West, built in 1909, was at one point the city's second largest high school. Its students, dressed in their distinctive green and white letter sweaters and jackets, were a familiar sight on the streets of Uptown. The local business community supported its local high school, and decorated the store windows for the school's homecoming. West's students provided a steady customer base for Uptown's many soda fountains and confectioners, as well as for its retail stores. Many of these same students also held after-school jobs in the local stores. When the school closed in 1982, Uptown was left without a high school of its own. Southwest, located at 47th and Beard, served the area's high school students.

Uptown offered a variety of other educational options in addition to its public schools. Business and secretarial schools existed in the second floors of Hennepin and Lake's commercial buildings. A fine arts school, Atelier Lack, was previously located near Hennepin and Lake. The Lakeland Dental Academy provided training to students in the former Uptown Ballroom building on Lake Street.

Calhoun School, located on Girard Avenue between Lake and 31st Streets, opened its doors to 200 students and six teachers in 1887. When the school opened, it became Minneapolis's 39th school, and brought the district-wide student enrollment to 17,997. Although an elementary school was needed in the neighborhood, some parents worried about potential transportation issues. These parents were concerned that it would be difficult for their children to later travel to Central High School. A newspaper article from 1887 reassured readers that their concerns were unwarranted: "This reporter was informed by authorities that as a business section is developed around Lake Street and Hennepin Avenue, more summer lake homes will be converted into year-round dwellings and farm lands will be divided into home-sites. The resulting population will necessitate public transportation as far South and as West as Lake Street and Hennepin Avenue." Ultimately the Hennepin-Lake area became very well-connected to the rest of the city via public transportation, and in 1909 West High opened, providing local students with their own high school. (Courtesy Hennepin History Museum.)

Further additions were made to Calhoun School in 1904 and in 1920. The 1904 addition doubled the number of classrooms, while the 1920 addition added 10 more classrooms. The building is shown here with its 1920s extension. The school was torn down in 1975 at a cost of $27,500. (Courtesy Minneapolis Public Schools.)

The original Calhoun School enrollment area ran from east of Lake of the Isles on 27th Street to Harriet Avenue; south on Harriet to Lake Street; west on Lake to Aldrich, south on Aldrich to 31st; west on 31st to Dupont, south on Dupont to 38th Street; west on 38th to Lakewood Cemetery; and bordered on the south and west by Lakewood, Lake Calhoun, and Lake of the Isles. The school's first six teachers were paid a base annual salary of $650. Their contracts allowed the school to terminate their employment if they married or were unable to pay their debts. In 1905, Calhoun School became one of four schools in Minneapolis to offer kindergarten, and in 1907, it became the first school in Minneapolis to organize a PTA. (Courtesy Minneapolis Public Schools.)

This large boiler played an essential role in Calhoun School. Its purchase was part of the building's total construction cost of $26,380. (Courtesy Minneapolis Public Schools.)

During the academic year 1922–1923, Calhoun's student enrollment peaked at 1,116. The following year, Calhoun's seventh and eighth graders moved to the new Jefferson Junior High, alleviating much of the school's overcrowding. In the 1924–1925 academic year, Calhoun School was chosen to serve as the site for "experimental demonstration instruction," advanced training for experienced Minneapolis teachers. (Courtesy Minneapolis Public Schools.)

This photograph, dating to the 1920s, was taken in what was then the newest portion of the Calhoun School building. The students shown here were participating in an eye exam in the school's gymnasium. The school did not get a gym until 1920; before that they used the facilities at Joyce Church across the street. (Courtesy Minneapolis Public Schools.)

70

These 1940 Calhoun students had the opportunity to learn first-hand about the making of honey. The University of Minnesota loaned the school a glass case to put in a classroom window. The case allowed bees to access the hive from the outside, and allowed the students to safely observe their activities from inside the classroom. (Courtesy Minneapolis Public Library.)

Between 1920 and 1932, eleven new junior high schools were built in Minneapolis, including Jefferson Junior High. Jefferson was built in 1923, with opening ceremonies held November 24, 1924. The first principal was Mr. A.E. MacQuarrie. Students could take courses in drawing, history, civics, home economics, Latin, manufacturing, math, and music, among other things. (Courtesy Minneapolis Public Schools.)

This unusual view of Jefferson was taken by the Minneapolis School Board c. 1923. "The Board of Education through its bureau of buildings has provided a plain, compact building splendidly designed for Junior High purposes," an observer noted in 1924, the year it opened to students. (Courtesy Minneapolis Public Schools.)

Although most of Jefferson's students lived within walking distance of the school, most of them chose to eat lunch in the cafeteria. Students could either bring a lunch from home or choose to purchase food at school. (Courtesy Minneapolis Public Schools.)

This photograph was taken shortly after construction at Jefferson was completed. The library's tables and chairs were in place, as were the bookshelves, but the students, staff, and books had yet to arrive. (Courtesy Minneapolis Public Schools.)

The Jefferson Junior High Glee Club frequently performed for neighborhood groups and for service clubs around the city. This 1925 club photo shows the members of the glee club, consisting of boys in grades seven through nine. (Courtesy Minneapolis Public Schools.)

West High was built in 1908 at a cost of $25,000. "The new West High School has been the magnet that has attracted nearly everyone located in the western and southern part of the city," reported the *Minneapolis Journal* that September. In 1908, 1,040 students began school at West, and in June of 1909, 108 students became the first to graduate from the new school. (Courtesy Minneapolis Public Schools.)

Students at West could take a wide variety of courses, ranging from the basics, such as English or History, to more specialized courses in electrical engineering and drafting. (Courtesy Minneapolis Public Schools.)

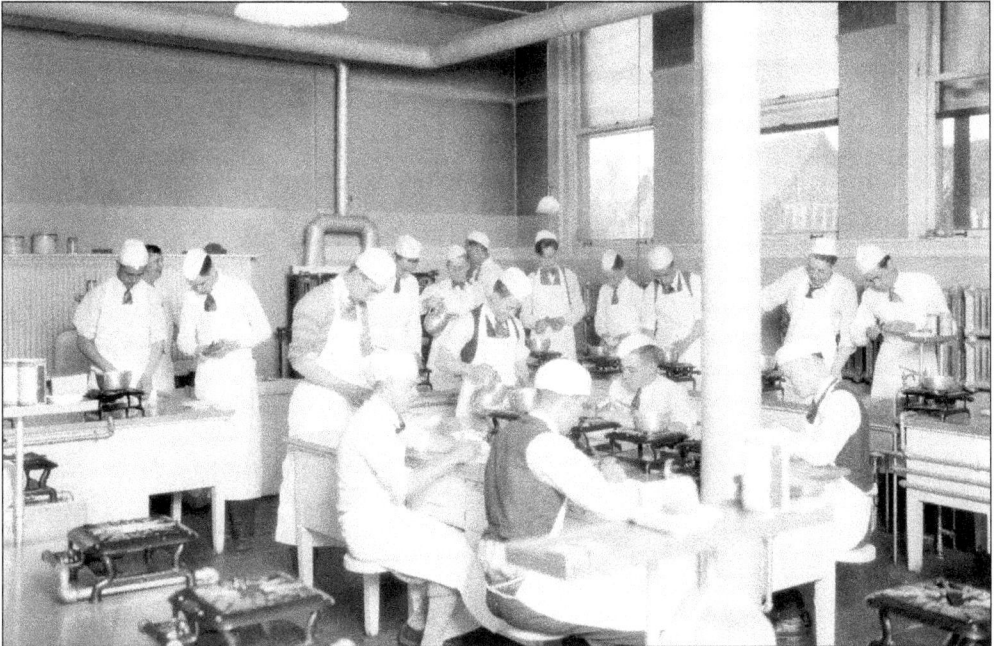

Courses such as cooking were gender-segregated at both Jefferson and West. In this male-only cooking class, boys learned the basics of kitchen skills, including the preserving of garden vegetables. (Courtesy Minneapolis Public Schools.)

The first annual West High School yearbook, the *Hesperian*, described West's auditorium as "the pride of the school" and the "greatest feature of the building." The unnamed authors described the room in glowing terms: "A large double swinging door on each side gives access from the side halls to the body of the house, while the balcony can be entered only by similar doors from the halls above. One enters and sees a great light hall with windows at sides and back. The walls and ceilings are dull, rough white, the woodwork polished pine. The whole makes a beautiful audience room, accommodating fifteen hundred people." (Courtesy Minneapolis Public Schools.)

This photograph, published in the first West *Hesperian*, the school's yearbook, shows the auditorium filled with students, perhaps taken at the rally held in honor of the *Hesperian*, held March 19, or at the talk given by Kenyon College's President Pierce, held March 29th. (Courtesy Thatcher Imboden.)

The students shown here inaugurated West's football program. The school's first season did not go well, with West losing five out of six games, but that was perhaps not unexpected with a brand-new team. None of the players had played together, and only two had previously played football at the high school level. Nevertheless, the team continued to grow stronger, and attracted more than 40 team members. Shown here are the team's coach, manager, and the school's first football players to be awarded the first football letters. Pictured are, from left to right: (seated) Joe Mattern, right end; Russell Stair, quarterback; and St. Matthew Clark, left end; (middle row) Carroll Coppage, right tackle; Floyd Langdon, right guard; Philip Lewis, captain; Clifford Pollock, left guard; and Earl Tumy, left tackle; (top row) Ben Parris, manager; Ralph Capron, left half; Clinton Webster, fullback; Carleton Burrier, coach; Noyes Bright, right half; Carl Lauritzen, substitute; and Paul Ash, substitute. (Courtesy Thatcher Imboden.)

Female students at West had many athletic options available to them, including field hockey, speedball, volleyball, baseball, hiking, horseback riding, swimming, tennis, tumbling, skating, and fencing. Shown here are some of the 16 members of the fencing club. Fencing was taught by Mr. Gerry Thomas, led by student Jane Watkins, and open to both male and female students. (Courtesy Thatcher Imboden.)

West offered highly specialized courses to its students. This student was photographed for the 1938 yearbook. (Courtesy Thatcher Imboden.)

Younger West graduates may not recognize this view of their school; the grassy area shown here was later converted into a parking lot. (Courtesy Minneapolis Public Library.)

West High School closed its doors in June of 1982 and was demolished in 1984. After its closing, most Uptown students moved to Southwest High School. (Courtesy Minneapolis Public Schools.)

Calhoun Secretarial School, shown here in the late 1930s, offered its students advanced training in secretarial skills. It was located on the second floor of 2933 Hennepin and offered both day and evening courses. The space was also used by other neighborhood organizations, including several of Temple Israel's religious classes during the 1920s. The school promised its students that "our graduates are making good," and boasted "our equipment is new and modern." Its students were active in the community, and could participate in extracurricular activities such as a glee club that frequently performed at local events. (Courtesy Thatcher Imboden.)

Shown here are four January 1945 graduates of the Electronic Television Institute, located at 2933 Hennepin. The school trained women to serve as radio traffic directors for national air lines. (Courtesy Minneapolis Public Library.)

Six

THE BUSINESS DISTRICT
1920–1940

The development of streetcar lines went hand in hand with the development of the Uptown area, as streetcars made it possible for new residents to live near the lakes and still commute to downtown jobs. As new homes for these permanent residents sprang up between 1900 and 1920, businesses quickly followed. The Hennepin-Lake intersection became a nucleus of development offering area residents all of life's amenities—cleaners, hardware stores, restaurants, theaters, schools, clothing stores, doctors, and nearly anything else imaginable. Hennepin Avenue, once designated a boulevard by the Park Board, had opened for commercial development in 1905. New streetcar lines, new homes, and Hennepin's emergence as a major Minneapolis commercial street led to Uptown's growth. Although the Hennepin-Lake intersection had housed commercial businesses since the late nineteenth century, its major development dates to the 1920s. Uptown's increasing population density, close proximity to the wealthy families living near the lakes, and accessibility to mass transportation made it an appealing location for businesses. Restaurants, movie theaters, the Fifth Northwestern Bank, and stores of all sorts opened during this time. New buildings, including a car dealership and plant in the Bryant Building on Hennepin and the elaborate Schlampp Building at Lagoon and Hennepin, were erected during this time. It was during the 1920s that Uptown became established as the premier retail district outside of downtown.

The 1930s were not as successful as the 1920s were for Uptown. The Depression years proved difficult for local businesses. The city directories list many buildings on Lake and Hennepin, the main commercial streets, as vacant. Despite the tough times, many Uptown businesses did survive, and the commercial district itself continued to develop and draw in visitors.

This 1930s view of Uptown shows the results of the dense development that occurred in the previous decade. Large buildings visible in this image include West High School and its athletic

fields, Calhoun Elementary School, the Minneapolis Arena, and the Buzza Building. (Courtesy Minneapolis Public Schools.)

Abdallah's was located at the northwest corner of the Lake and Hennepin intersection. Syrian immigrants Albert and Helen Abdallah started the candy store and soda fountain in 1909. The store's chocolates and other candies were made in large copper kettles using traditional recipes. In addition to sweets and soda fountain treats, Abdallah's also sold lunches and dinners. The company still exists today, although no longer at its Hennepin and Lake location. (Courtesy Minneapolis Public Library.)

This 1920s view of 3005 Hennepin, a three-story building located just south of Lake Street, shows the wide variety of stores and businesses that coexisted at the intersection of Hennepin and Lake. A hardware store, fruit store, massage parlor, music school, and several doctors shared this building. 3005 Hennepin was destroyed by a four-alarm fire in June of 1975. The fire displaced several stores and offices, a ballet school, an art school, and one apartment. (Courtesy Minneapolis Public Library.)

The Carling Hotel, located at 29th and Hennepin, was built in 1925 at a cost of $100,000. The ground floor's two shop spaces contained a cafeteria on one side and the Federal Bakery on the other. "Hotel" was a legal distinction—Minneapolis law defined a hotel as a building with mostly rooms for sleeping only, with at least 15 rooms above the first floor, and food provided in a "general dining room or café." Residents at the Carling lived in the upper floors in one of 50 rooms complete with private baths. They had their meals in the downstairs cafeteria or in one of the area's many restaurants and cafés. (Courtesy Minneapolis Public Library.)

John Schmidlers' meats and groceries store was located on the northeast corner of Hennepin and Lake during the 1920s and early 1930s. The intersection is shown here in the early 1930s, shortly before the five-cluster light poles lining Lake Street were replaced as part of Lake Street's "White Way" program. The goal was to bathe the length of Lake Street with clear, bright light. The merchants at Hennepin and Lake were the first in the city to implement the new lights, replacing these older light posts in the spring of 1931. (Courtesy Hennepin History Museum.)

The local meat and grocery chain Witt's had a long history in Minneapolis; the first Witt's opened downtown in 1888. This photograph was taken of the Witt's store located at 2210 Hennepin in the mid-1930s. (Courtesy Minneapolis Public Library.)

The Calhoun Realty Company played a significant role in the development of the Uptown area. Owner Fred Lohman first encountered the Calhoun Realty Company when he stopped in the office in an attempt to sell the owner sugar beet stock. She declined purchasing the stock, and instead convinced him to purchase the business. Shown here is the Calhoun Realty office in 1925; Fred Lohman is the man holding the telephone in the lower right corner. (Courtesy Charles "Zeke" Koehler.)

Prior to the 1950s, Lagoon Avenue did not slice through Hennepin Avenue. This photograph, taken in the mid-1920s, shows some of the buildings on the site currently occupied by McDonald's. These included Hove's grocery store, prior to its move to Lake Street, Berry's meat market, and Thomson's bakery offering "fine pastry." (Courtesy Hennepin History Museum.)

In 1922, Russell Lund began work at the Hove's grocery store at Lake and Hennepin. Lund was a dedicated employee, and within three months had become a partner in the cheese and cracker department. He later developed a pre-popped and packaged popcorn line, named Red E Popt Popcorn Company, to be sold at the store. Using his popcorn profits he later purchased and built a new Hove's store located on Lake Street, where the current Lunds still stands. In 1939, Russell Lund became a full partner in the perishable food department. (Courtesy Lunds Foods.)

In 1902 Peter Hove opened the first Hove's grocery store at 1203 Glenwood Avenue. He opened a Lake and Hennepin store in 1918. During the 1920s, Hove's was located on Hennepin Avenue in a warren of four separate stores connected by doors. In 1939, Hove's employee Russell T. Lund purchased land on West Lake Street for $40,000. He knocked down several apartment buildings and built a new grocery store on the site. He signed a 25-year lease with Hove for the new store, one of the Twin Cities' first self-service grocery stores. The new store included a parking lot for customers, although the primary entrance still faced the sidewalk. (Courtesy Lunds Foods.)

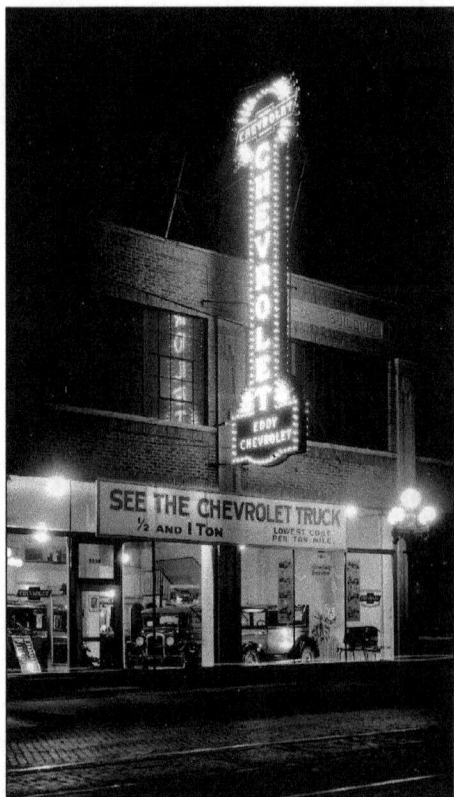

This image shows the Bryant Building, located at 3032–3038 Hennepin. In 1923 the *Lake District Advocate* published an article entitled "S.W. Eddy's New Ford Garage at Lake St. and Hennepin Avenue Finest Plant of Kind in Northwest," detailing the wonders of the new building. "One cannot help but be impressed with the beauty and massiveness embodied in the exterior of the building," wrote the reporter, "in fact it is one of the finest appearing buildings we have seen for some time. . . . On entering the show room you are confronted with a large space decorated in most artistic manner with stairways leading up to a mezzanine floor on either side. On the mezzanine we found the sales and general offices. The general effect of the show room and offices is most pleasing to the eye." The service department was located in the rear of the building. Another shop, located on the second floor, was where cars "were carefully inspected and tested to make sure that everything was as it should be." Fifty employees worked at Eddy's. Throughout the 1930s, this dealership was owned and operated by former University of Minnesota football star Bert Baston. (Courtesy Minnesota Historical Society.)

This gas station, located at Lake Street and Holmes, is shown in 1939. By the 1930s the Uptown area was home to a large variety of automobile-related businesses; car dealerships, garages, auto accessory stores, and a large number of gas stations, needed to keep residents' cars filled and running. (Courtesy Minneapolis Public Library.)

Kenwood 2674

THE JOHNSON
Pure
MILK CO., INC

FRESH BUTTER and BUTTERMILK
CHURNED DAILY

PURE PASTEURIZED MILK
and CREAM

2824 Emerson Ave. So.

C. J. E. Johnson, Pres.   Minneapolis, Minn.

The Johnson Milk Company, located at 28th Street and Emerson, was just one of many dairies operating within the Uptown area. Local residents received fresh milk daily. Many older local apartment buildings still retain windows leading from their apartments into the hallway—the milkmen placed the fresh milk into this space, where it could be easily retrieved by the residents within. (Courtesy Hennepin History Museum.)

This window, created by Professional Pharmacy in conjunction with National Pharmacy Week, was meant to remind customers that medicine revolved around science. The annual National Pharmacy Week was created by the American Pharmacists Association in 1925 with a goal to "promote the value of pharmacy services." The annual event was usually given a theme: the 1935 window display highlights the contrast between superstitions and science. (Courtesy Hennepin History Museum.)

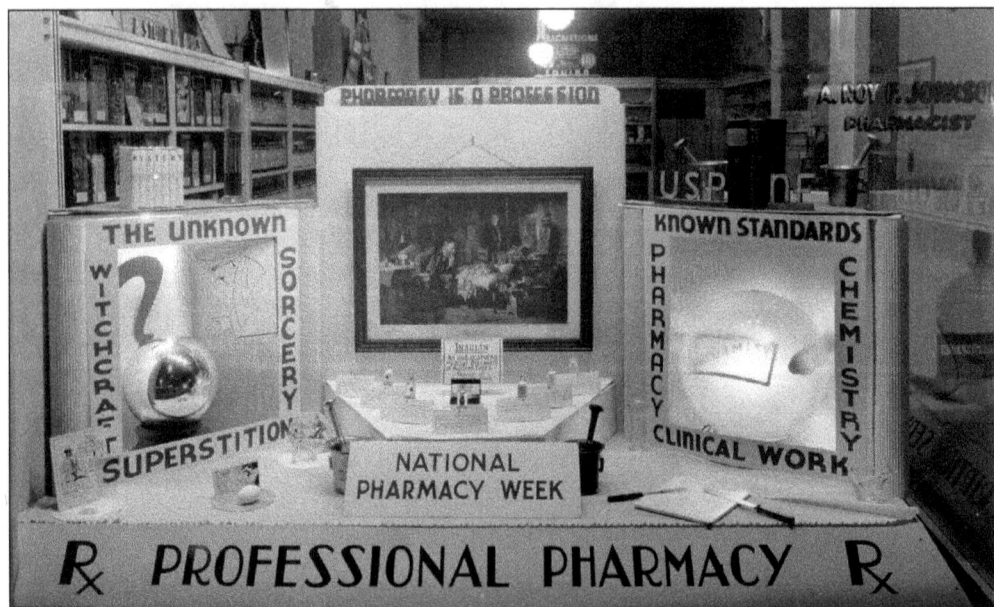

Professional Pharmacy, located at Irving and Lake, was owned and operated by Roy F. Johnson. The business first appears in city directories in 1936, suggesting that these 1935 photographs were commissioned for its opening. Pharmacies were a familiar sight to area residents. "There was a pharmacy every two blocks," recounted Rose Roberts, the former owner of another local pharmacy located on 28th and Hennepin. (Courtesy Hennepin History Museum.)

Schlampp & Son Inc., the Northwest's largest furrier, moved to the Uptown area in the early 1920s. The Schlampp building contained first floor retail space and a workshop, while the second floor served as office space. Architect H.J. Scherey included special features for the protection of furs from both fire and theft. Schlampp significantly expanded the building in 1929, and also built an adjacent storage building facing what is now Lagoon. The 1929 renovations were overseen by architects Liebenberg and Kaplan, also known for their work on the Granada Theater, the Uptown Theater, Temple Israel, and Adath Jeshurun. More than 95 percent of the garments sold in the store were manufactured on the premises. The storage of furs was another significant part of business; fur requires cold storage, and residents of every state in the United States as well as several foreign countries stored their furs at Schlampp's in the off-season. (Courtesy Minnesota Historical Society.)

Local resident and West graduate Zeke Koehler had deep family ties with the Uptown area; his uncle Fred Lohman had owned Calhoun Realty since the 1920s. Like many area residents, Koehler lived and worked in the area, holding jobs as advertising manager at Schlampp Furs, as a salesman for Sim's Men's Wear, and as a "bag boy" at Hove's grocery store at the time when Russell Lund was the meat department manager. Koehler was active in local business associations. (Courtesy Charles "Zeke" Koehler.)

91

A wide variety of businesses were located near the 29th Street railroad corridor tracks, including lumberyards, steel yards, dairies, stables, factories, the Buzza greeting card company, and other assorted manufacturers. Some of the land later became the Mall. (Courtesy Minneapolis Park Board.)

The Buzza Company was first founded in 1907 and specialized in poster production. After a downturn in the demand for posters, the company turned to manufacturing more financially lucrative greeting cards. In 1917 founder George Buzza expanded the company's offerings and instated a new generous return policy; the result was an explosion in business. Buzza's 1917 sales were $75,000; two years later sales had reached nearly $200,000, and by the early 1920s they were in the low millions. The company purchased a building on Lake Street between Dupont and Colfax to accommodate this growth. The new building and its subsequent renovations and additions could handle Buzza's high level of production. "The American public is buying more everyday greeting cards than ever before," announced George Buzza. The company merged with the Charles C. Clark Company of New York in 1928, making the new Buzza-Clark Company the second-largest greeting card and art publishing company in the United States. Sales began to decline in the late 1920s, although the company survived until 1942, at which point it closed and the building at Dupont and Colfax was sold. (Courtesy Minneapolis Public Library.)

The creation of Buzza greeting cards, calendars, and other publications was a strictly regulated process. Designers, usually trained male artists, thought up and created the images. The term "artists" was used to refer to the people who painted the cards. These were usually young women between the ages of 18 and 25. Their job required a steady hand, and an attention to detail, but did not allow for creativity or artistic expression. (Courtesy Minneapolis Public Library.)

As was common in the 1920s, many Buzza jobs were gender-segregated. These women are some of Buzza's 300 employees. Many different tasks were undertaken at the Buzza complex, also known as Craftacres; designers, printers, artists, assembly workers, office staff, storage and shipping employees, and salesmen all worked at the building. "Within the last fifteen years Minneapolis has forged ahead as a manufacturing center for greeting cards, calendars, and other types of colored novelties," the Minneapolis Public Schools advised graduates. "In the manufacturing of greeting cards, Minneapolis is one of the leading centers in the United States." (Courtesy Minneapolis Public Library.)

The Buzza building was built in 1907 as the Self-Threading Needle Company building. It was purchased by the Buzza Company in 1923. They proceeded to renovate and add to the building as the company grew, constructing three major additions in just four years. These additions included a three-story section facing Colfax, a four-story section on the north, and the six-story tower emblazoned with the Buzza name on Dupont. The renovations were designed by Magney, Tusler, and Setter, the same architects that designed Foshay Tower. After Buzza closed in 1942, the building was purchased by the War Department and used by Honeywell as a manufacturing space for precision optical instruments for the army. Between 1945 and 1950 the building was used by the veterans' administration, and in 1950 the building became the headquarters of the Minnesota military district and took on the nickname "Little Pentagon." The Minneapolis Public Schools acquired the building from the federal government in 1971, and dedicated it as the Florence M. Lehmann Education Center in 1973. (Courtesy Minneapolis Public Library.)

My Friend

I could sail the waters of all the world,
    Bitter and wild and blue
And never I'd find a friend to love
    Like the friend I've found in you.

I could walk down all the roads of the world,
    And knock on the doors forever
And never I'd find a friend like you,
    Never ~ Never ~ Never !

J. P. McEvoy

This card, produced on thick card stock and printed with multiple colors, was produced by the Buzza Company in 1925. Buzza had started producing cards with 24 colors as early as 1909. The company became known for their daring use of color, and for the quality of design. This card has an embossed design with a raised verse by the writer J.P. McEvoy. This is just one version produced by Buzza of the same verse; they also produced similar work in different formats suitable for framing. (Courtesy Thatcher Imboden.)

Buzza's large complex housed offices, studios, and storage space. "This firm annually carries the name of Minneapolis to 40,000,000 homes and business establishments," reported the *Tribune* in 1923. Buzza's location off of the 29th Street industrial corridor made it easy for railroad transportation of their cards. (Courtesy Minneapolis Public Library.)

The upper portion of the Buzza building's six-story tower was decorated with Renaissance furnishings from an Italian villa. The space was meant to be inspirational for company designers, salesmen, and management, and impressive to visitors. (Courtesy Minneapolis Public Library.)

Seven

THE BUSINESS DISTRICT 1940–1970

The 1940s, 1950s, and 1960s brought still more changes to the Uptown area. Following World War II, Uptown's businesses faced increasing competition from the suburbs. Some businesses were able to adapt to a shifting society. The Hove's grocery store moved to a new location on Lake Street, where a new modern supermarket and an adjoining parking lot were built—conveniences demanded by the changing times. Uptown still offered something that could not be found in Southdale or the other Dales, and retained its vitality. The area became known as one of the best places to go for restaurants and evening entertainment.

Uptown started to lose some of its prestige during the 1960s. In 1964, a group of local business men and women came together to create the Uptown Art Fair. The Uptown Art Fair was intended to promote interest in the Hennepin-Lake shopping area and revitalize the energy of the area. Throughout the 1960s, Uptown continued to gain a reputation as an "artsy" neighborhood. Uptown, while still fashionable, was less glamorous than it had been in previous decades, but remained a popular destination.

The Irwin Building on Lake Street was completed in June of 1923. The *Lake District Advocate* reported that "it has been designed for stores and offices, and will be a wonderful addition and credit to the corner." Businesses occupying the building in 1946, when this photo was taken, included Kathleen Frocks, Thomas' Jewel Box, dentist Dr. Downing, and a beauty salon. The building next door housed the Uptown Insurance Agency. Their decision to incorporate "Uptown" into their name reflects the identification of the term "Uptown" with the Hennepin and Lake area. (Courtesy Minnesota Historical Society.)

The Uptown business community supported the annual holiday decorating of the Hennepin-Lake intersection. The seasonal lights of the business district blended with the streetlights, store signs, billboards, and lit-up restaurant and store interiors to illuminate the neighborhood. On the right side of the photograph are the Uptown Theater and the Rainbow Cafe; on the left is the Chapman Graham Ice Cream Company. Chapman Graham was known for its quality catering in addition to its ice cream, and many of Minneapolis's most famous hosts and hostesses depended on them for holiday party catering. (Courtesy Minnesota Historical Society.)

The Rainbow Café, located on the western side of Hennepin between Lake Street and Lagoon, began its long tenure in 1919. Founder Christ Legeros came to Minneapolis from Milwaukee; while working as a busboy there he broke some dishes and "lit out of town to Minneapolis." The Café became a Minneapolis institution and was a destination for 750,000 hungry diners from across the region annually. Following World War II, the second generation of Minneapolis Legeroses joined the family business. The large overhanging Rainbow Café sign, shown in this 1952 photograph, was later removed when the city instated new building codes. (Courtesy John Legeros.)

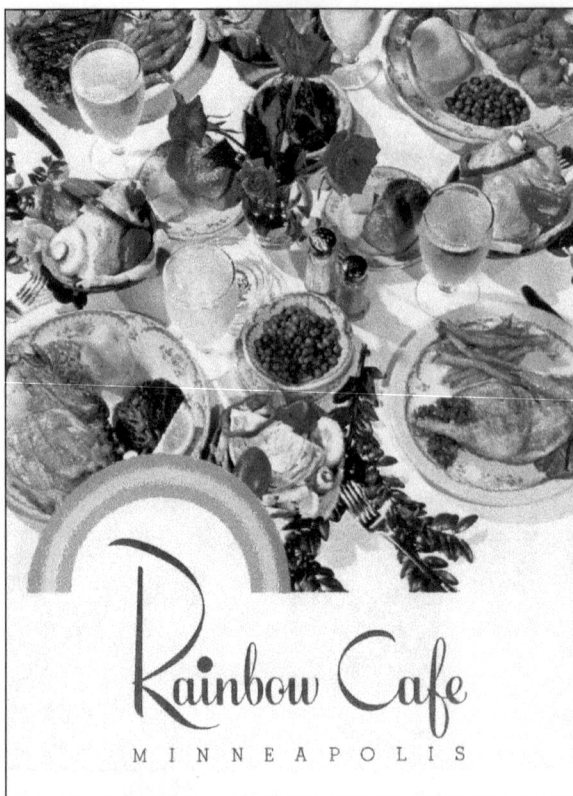

This menu dates from the early 1950s. In 1954, Rainbow patrons could dine on french-fried half-spring chicken for $2.25 or breaded veal cutlet for $1.85, and finish the meal with a cup of coffee for 10¢. Diners could also chose from a Chinese section of the menu offering chow mein or fried rice, popular dishes of the time. The café remained open until 2:30 a.m., attracting diners after nights spent at the area's many theaters or ballrooms. The menu was created with the help of a commercial photographer specializing in food. This menu will be familiar to several generations of Rainbow patrons; the cover was used until the Legeros family sold the café in 1979. The menu changed daily, and in the interest of saving money and paper, the colorful menu cover was plastic-coated and the daily menu was printed on plain white paper and inserted separately. (Courtesy Tian Barbatsis Dayton.)

Pictured here from left to right are Christ Legeros, Ann Grega, Myrtle Chambers, and Elmer Floback. Christ Legeros, pouring the metaxa, was the founder and owner of the Rainbow Café. Ann Grega and Myrtle Chambers both worked in the café. Elmer Floback was a member of the Uptown Commercial Club, as was host Christ Legeros. This 1954 holiday party was held at the Rainbow Café. (Courtesy John Legeros.)

From left to right are Ed Schlampp Sr., Mr. Wohler, Christ Legeros (serving), Russell Thayer, and Russell Spear. Ed Schlampp owned Schlampp Furs, and Mr. Wohler owned the Wohler Hardware on Hennepin. Russell Spears owned the Acme Awning Company, the company that supplied many local homes and businesses with custom commercial and residential awnings. Russell Thayer was the president of the Fifth Northwestern Bank. This photo was taken at Christ Legeros' Rainbow Café. (Courtesy John Legeros.)

HONOR GUESTS

Governor and Mrs. Orville L. Freeman — Senator and Mrs. H. H. Humphrey
President Meredith Wilson — Mayor and Mrs. P. K. Peterson
Mr. and Mrs. Ike Armstrong — Mr. and Mrs. Murray Warmath — Denver Crawford
Mr. and Mrs. Jim Kelly — Mr. and Mrs. Bert Baston — George "Butch" Nash
Jim Camp — Dick Larson — Dick Borstad — Robert Bossons — Wally Johnson

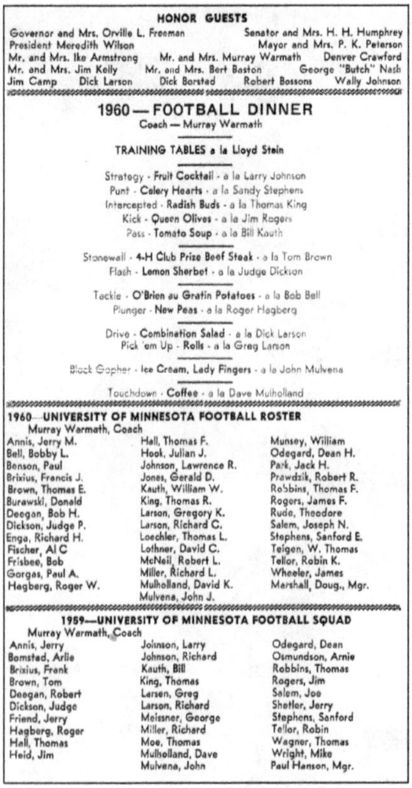

1960 — FOOTBALL DINNER
Coach — Murray Warmath

TRAINING TABLES a la Lloyd Stein

Strategy - **Fruit Cocktail** - a la Larry Johnson
Punt - **Celery Hearts** - a la Sandy Stephens
Intercepted - **Radish Buds** - a la Thomas King
Kick - **Queen Olives** - a la Jim Rogers
Pass - **Tomato Soup** - a la Bill Kauth

Stonewall - **4-H Club Prize Beef Steak** - a la Tom Brown
Flash - **Lemon Sherbet** - a la Judge Dickson

Tackle - **O'Brien au Gratin Potatoes** - a la Bob Bell
Plunger - **New Peas** - a la Roger Hagberg

Drive - **Combination Salad** - a la Dick Larson
Pick 'em Up - **Rolls** - a la Greg Larson

Black Gopher - **Ice Cream, Lady Fingers** - a la John Mulvena

Touchdown - **Coffee** - a la Dave Mulholland

1960—UNIVERSITY OF MINNESOTA FOOTBALL ROSTER
Murray Warmath, Coach

Annis, Jerry M.	Hall, Thomas F.	Munsey, William
Bell, Bobby L.	Hook, Julian J.	Odegard, Dean H.
Benson, Paul	Johnson, Lawrence R.	Park, Jack H.
Brixius, Francis J.	Jones, Gerald D.	Prawdzik, Robert R.
Brown, Thomas E.	Kauth, William W.	Robbins, Thomas F.
Burawski, Donald	King, Thomas R.	Rogers, James F.
Deegan, Bob H.	Larson, Gregory K.	Rude, Theodore
Dickson, Judge P.	Larson, Richard C.	Salem, Joseph N.
Enga, Richard H.	Loechler, Thomas L.	Stephens, Sanford E.
Fischer, Al C	Lothner, David C.	Teigen, W. Thomas
Frisbee, Bob	McNeil, Robert L.	Tellor, Robin K.
Gorgas, Paul A.	Miller, Richard L.	Wheeler, James
Hagberg, Roger W.	Mulholland, David K.	Marshall, Doug., Mgr.
	Mulvena, John J.	

1959—UNIVERSITY OF MINNESOTA FOOTBALL SQUAD
Murray Warmath, Coach

Annis, Jerry	Johnson, Larry	Odegard, Dean
Bomstad, Arlie	Johnson, Richard	Osmundson, Arnie
Brixius, Frank	Kauth, Bill	Robbins, Thomas
Brown, Tom	King, Thomas	Rogers, Jim
Deegan, Robert	Larsen, Greg	Salem, Joe
Dickson, Judge	Larson, Richard	Shetler, Jerry
Friend, Jerry	Meissner, George	Stephens, Sanford
Hagberg, Roger	Miller, Richard	Tellor, Robin
Hall, Thomas	Moe, Thomas	Wagner, Thomas
Heid, Jim	Mulholland, Dave	Wright, Mike
	Mulvena, John	Paul Hanson, Mgr.

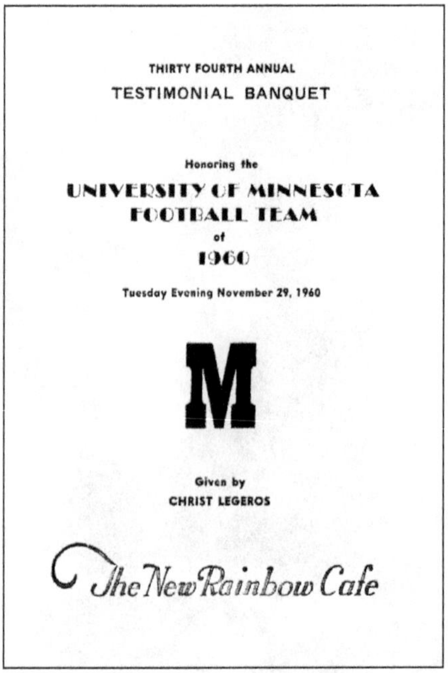

THIRTY FOURTH ANNUAL
TESTIMONIAL BANQUET

Honoring the
UNIVERSITY OF MINNESOTA
FOOTBALL TEAM
of
1960

Tuesday Evening November 29, 1960

M

Given by
CHRIST LEGEROS

The New Rainbow Cafe

"The 1960 season will always be remembered as the biggest turnaround in the history of Minnesota football," reminisces the University of Minnesota. The Gophers had finished the 1959 season 2–7 overall and last in the Big 10. In 1960 the team attended the Rose Bowl for the first time ever, and finished the season 8–2 overall, 6–1 in the Big Ten. The annual Gopher football event pictured above was held in November 1960 at Uptown's Rainbow Cafe. In addition to the team members and coaches, other invited guests included Governor Freeman and his wife, Senator Humphrey and Mrs. Humphrey, the mayor of Minneapolis, and a selection of other local, state, and university dignitaries. Rather than appetizers and main courses, the guests enjoyed "intercepted radish buds a la Thomas King," "pick-em-up rolls a la Greg Larson," and "touchdown coffee a la Dave Mullholland." (Courtesy Michael John Legeros.)

The Hull Dobbs Company, based in Memphis, Tennessee, began in 1937 and was the largest Ford dealership in the world by 1942. At one point, Dobbs dealerships sold one-quarter of all Fords sold in the United States. This photograph was taken in November of 1954, and shows the Dobbs dealership on Hennepin and 26th, just one of several Twin Cities Dobbs dealerships. The location itself had long been a car dealership, and 10 years earlier the Calhoun Motor Company advertised themselves as part of the "World's Largest Ford Dealer." (Courtesy Minnesota Historical Society.)

The three businesses shown here, Sim's on the corner, the Rainbow Café in the middle, and Marna Lee on the far right, were well-known neighborhood establishments. Sim's Haberdashery was known for its quality men's clothing and superb service; Dayton's sent their salesmen there to learn about customer service. After opening in 1919, the Rainbow Café had grown to become a landmark of the corner. Marna Lee was a popular local women's clothing store. This photograph was taken in September of 1967. (Courtesy John Legeros.)

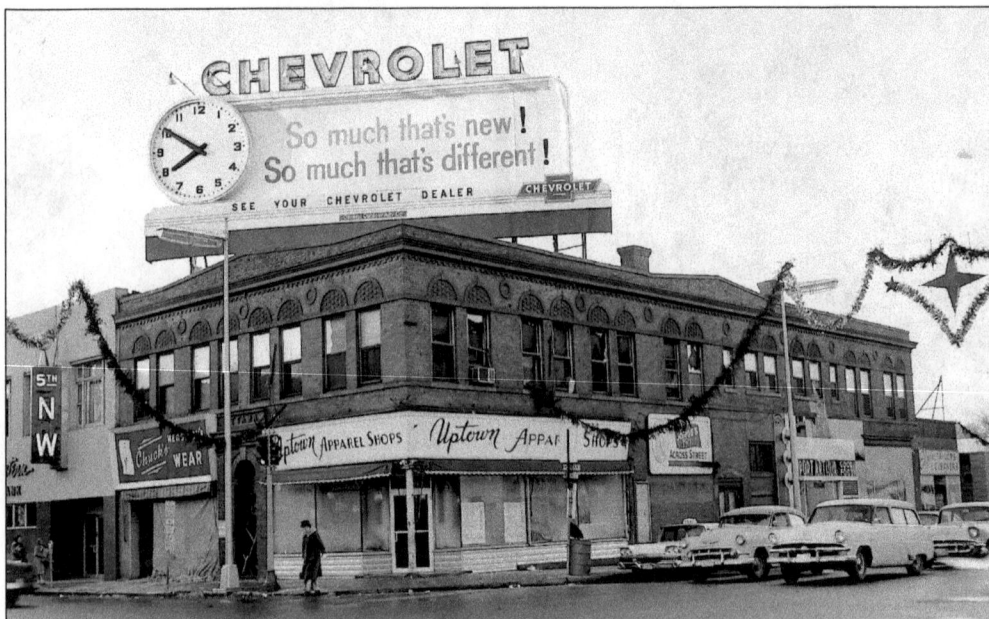

The southwest corner of Hennepin and Lake, shown here in 1959, was home to a variety of businesses. Businesses familiar to longtime Uptown residents include the Fifth Northwestern Bank and the Port Arthur Café, both visible in this photograph. Fifth Northwestern Bank, later Norwest and most recently Wells Fargo, came to Uptown in the late 1920s at the request of local merchants. The bank left its Hennepin location in 1962 when it moved to the new Sons of Norway building on Lake Street. Port Arthur was known for its Chinese food, and was just one of many restaurants that thrived in the Uptown business district. (Courtesy Minnesota Historical Society.)

Morris and Christie Market is pictured here at the corner of 31st and Hennepin. It was founded by Chris Christie and Isadore Morris. The neighborhood grocery was particularly well known for its Greek food, popular with the many Greek families living in the Uptown area. (Courtesy Charles "Zeke" Koehler.)

In the 1950s or early 1960s Hove's remodeled its building, moving the entrance to the corner of the building, where it was equally accessible to visitors arriving both from the sidewalk and from the parking lot. A large towering marquis was built above the door. The large size of both the store's name, as well as its location, "Lake Street," emphasized that this store was part of the overall family of Hove's stores. The store continued to use their traditional slogan, "lowest average price everyday." (Courtesy Lunds Foods.)

Former Hove's employee Russell Lund became the owner of the now-familiar Lunds stores in 1964. Three years prior to the expiration of Hove's Lake Street store lease, Lund began making offers to purchase the business and the Hove's name. Negotiations were unsuccessful, and after February of 1963 Lund took ownership of the Lake Street store and changed its name to Lunds. Advertisements from the time promised customer the same quality and service offered by Hove's, reassuring them that the only thing changing was the name. (Courtesy Lunds Foods.)

Hove's slogan was "Lowest average price everyday." The former Hove's became known as not only a good place to do grocery shopping, but also as a good place to meet single men and women. "Although most people go to Lunds for groceries, some have found it's an equally good place to socialize," reported the *Minneapolis Star* in 1978. One happy shopper remarked "you can buy meat and meet girls all at the same time!" (Courtesy Lunds Foods.)

This 1964 photograph shows the new Lunds in the foreground and a car wash in the distance. The car wash was operated by Conn Legeros and was torn down in 1979 to make room for the construction of a building that now houses retail stores. Lunds had only recently changed ownership from Hove's; note that the Lunds sign has been very recently placed on top of the Hove's sign. (Courtesy Lunds Foods.)

Eight

THE BUSINESS DISTRICT
*1970–*TODAY

The 1970s brought significant changes to the Uptown business district. Several historic buildings were torn down for new development. These included the buildings occupying the northwest corner of Lagoon and Hennepin, demolished to make room for the new Walker Branch Library, and the Bonhus Hardware Building, located on the southeast corner of Lagoon and Hennepin, torn down and replaced with a freestanding McDonald's. The 1975 demolition of the Calhoun Elementary School created a gaping hole on Girard between Lake Street and 31st Street.

The early 1980s brought still more significant changes to Uptown's business core. Calhoun Square had been approved in the late 1970s, and construction began in the early 1980s. Many long-time businesses were forced to relocate during this period. Calhoun Square's ambitious plans included taking several historic buildings and incorporating them, together with new construction, into a single larger building. Calhoun Square sat partially on the site of the former Calhoun School and its grounds.

During the 1990s, the commercial character of Uptown changed further as large national retail chains entered the neighborhood. When the building on the southwest corner of Hennepin and Lake was destroyed by fire in the early 1990s, it was replaced by a new building housing the Gap. Other national chains that entered the district during this decade included Express and Urban Outfitters. Despite ongoing fears of suburbanization, the same fears first expressed when Calhoun Square was suggested, Uptown has thus far managed to successfully maintain a mix of national chains and independent stores. Calhoun Square, too, has changed with the times. Its offerings have evolved, but it has managed to survive and thrive. In recent years Uptown has once again become known as one of the Twin Cities' restaurant centers and entertainment spots.

The Legeros family is
shown here enjoying
dinner at the Rainbow
Café in 1970.
(Courtesy Patricia
Pennington Idstrom.)

The Rainbow Café had long maintained a large billboard atop its building. This billboard,
featuring two Guernsey cows, reminded patrons of the Rainbow's famous high-fat creamy milk.
The sign was put up in the 1940s or 1950s, and remained through the early 1970s. The neon
sign was visible from a far distance, and could be seen from the west side of Lake Calhoun. The
Rainbow Café purchased their milk from the Ewald Dairy Company, which advertised their
milk as coming from Golden Guernsey cows. The Golden Guernsey cow sign was the only
billboard to sit atop the Rainbow building. (Courtesy Ray Harris.)

The Sir Winston's Char Broil Restaurant building was torn down in the 1970s to make room for the new Walker Library. (Courtesy Ray Harris.)

Uptown residents might remember the distinctive mural painted on the side of Von's Superette at the intersection of Hennepin and 34th Street. The building now houses a Dunn Brothers. (Courtesy Michael Lander.)

McDonald's purchased the site at 2929 Hennepin in 1970. Several buidings, including the Bonhus Hardware building, were demolished to make room for the new restaurant. Local business owners worried that the building would detract from the pedestrian-oriented commercial district. The McDonald's was built with an outdoor patio alongside the Hennepin Avenue sidewalk; it was this dining area that became a popular destination for local teenagers often referred to as "McPunks" during the 1980s. Denny Teufel took over the McDonald's in 1984, and made changes aimed at transforming McDonald's from a premier punk hangout. "I want to try to make it a McFamily Store and not a McPunk store," he told the City Paper in 1985. To this end he renovated the outdoor patio, adding shrubbery, flowers, and a fence. The McDonald's shown here was torn down in 1996 to make room for a new building. The current restaurant sits close to the sidewalk, and an adjoining police substation fills in the gap that previously existed between the restaurant and its nearest neighbors. (Courtesy Ray Harris.)

The National grocery store and Walgreen's drugstore sit on the site of the former Minneapolis Arena at 29th Street between Dupont and Lagoon. The arena, an automobile repair shop and a commercial building containing several upholstery shops and a restaurant, were torn down to make room for the new shopping center dominated by new property owners National Food Store and its large parking lot in 1966. (Courtesy Ray Harris.)

This building on the north side of Lake Street between Girard and Fremont Avenues housed Cook Paint, Judy's Salon, and Red Wing Shoe Store. This building has since been demolished. (Courtesy Ray Harris.)

Sons of Norway, a Minneapolis-based fraternal benefit society, built its international headquarters at Lake Street and Humboldt in 1962. Also housed in the building was the Fifth Northwestern Bank, previously located at 3006 Hennepin. (Courtesy Ray Harris.)

This building on the southwest corner of Hennepin and Lake was built in 1910. The building's occupants included a Ligget's drugstore in the 1920s, a Hallmark shop and the Sample Hut in the 1970s, a novelty shop called Stars Unlimited in the late 1980s, and a Black's Photo store in the early 1990s. Fashion Corner occupied the former drugstore space beginning in 1977. After a fire destroyed the property in 1991, a new building housing the Gap was built. (Courtesy Ray Harris.)

Gas stations have long been a familiar sight in Uptown. This station at 28th and Hennepin was photographed in the mid-1970s. West High School is visible on the far right. (Courtesy Ray Harris.)

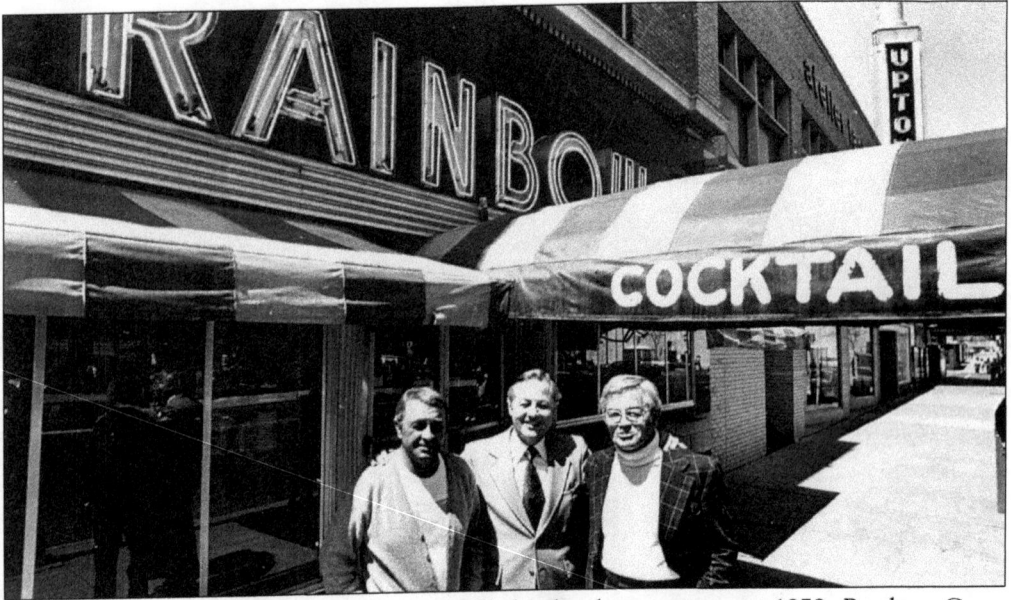

The Legeros family made the decision to sell the family restaurant in 1979. Brothers Conn Legeros, John Legeros, and George Legeros, shown here in August 1979, had long been active in Uptown's business community. The Rainbow continued under new ownership until closing for good in the 1980s. (Courtesy Tian Barbatsis Dayton.)

RAINBOW HOUSE

In 1979 the Legeros family sold the Rainbow building to Norm Ackerberg and the café to Bob Sabes. Sabes had community connections himself, having attended Calhoun, Jefferson, and West schools. Ackerberg announced a plan for renovations of the building, which he hoped would make better use of the space while maintaining square footage. These alterations, including the installation of an elevator shaft in the former space of the café's Art Deco bar, led to structural changes in the café; Sabes' redecoration of the café included the transformation from an Art Deco interior to a more modern one. The upper levels of the building itself were transformed from small apartments and several offices into expanded office and retail space, and skylights, an atrium, and a new awnings were added. The building's leasing agent, Joe McCormick, described the changes as "the most significant renovations to date in the Hennepin-Lake area in size and scope." (Courtesy Tian Barbatsis Dayton.)

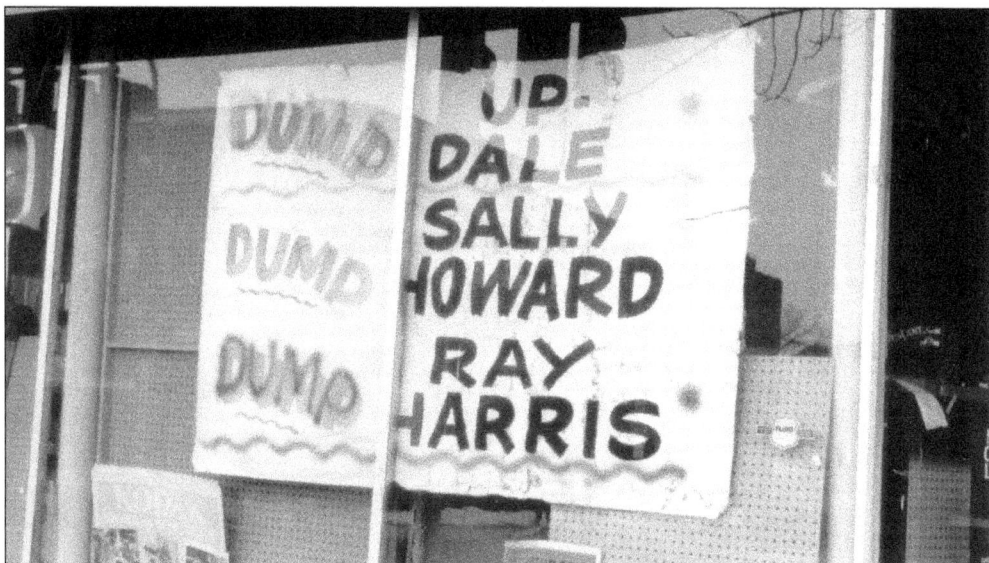

The creation of Calhoun Square involved large amounts of controversy and public debate. To get bond funding for the project, the Minneapolis City Council voted 12 to one to officially designate the Hennepin-Lake area "blighted." Some local residents and business owners feared the proposed development would lead to the suburbanization of Uptown and gave the proposed Calhoun Square the derisive name "Updale." Sally Howard was the Tenth Ward alderman at the time, and Ray Harris was the developer of Calhoun Square. (Courtesy Ray Harris.)

Calhoun Square held its grand opening in February 1984 after beginning construction in January 1983. Shown from left to right are Mayor Don Fraser, Calhoun Square developer Ray Harris, and council members Barbara Carlson, Joan Neimiec, and Sally Howard. (Courtesy Ray Harris.)

Architects Paul Pink and Associates created Calhoun Square out of a blend of old and new construction. Of the five buildings originally standing on the site, two were torn down and three were renovated to create the final space. The retained buildings include the Save-Mart building at the corner of Hennepin and Lake, the former post office farther down Hennepin, and part of the bowling alley at the southern end of the project. (Courtesy Ray Harris.)

Is this an example of Uptown's agricultural heritage continuing to the present day? The sight of a cow standing just feet away from the busy Hennepin-Lake intersection is not a familiar one. This cow is participating in a Kemps promotion in the early 1990s. (Courtesy Ray Harris.)

Calhoun Square's airy interior houses a wide variety of retail stores and businesses. Some of Calhoun Square's earliest stores had previously been located in the Hennepin-Lake business district, while others were new to the corner. (Courtesy Ray Harris.)

The March 13, 1991 fire that destroyed the building on the southwest corner of Hennepin and Lake was ignited by a spark from a plumber's torch being used in a second floor apartment. The fire quickly grew in size, and early attempts to stop the flames were unsuccessful. A total of 55 firefighters with 15 fire trucks fought the fire and managed to mostly contain it within the site. Kimson Vietnamese Restaurant, Fashion Corner, Gabriela's Vintage Clothing and Jewelry, Black's Photography, and three smaller businesses were left without a home, as were six residents of the apartments. The fire did $1.5 million in damage, although fortunately no one was injured. (Courtesy Ray Harris.)

Nine

ENTERTAINMENT

Movie theaters have been an important part of Uptown's entertainment heritage for much of the twentieth century. These theaters initially offered stages for vaudeville shows, as well as screens for silent movies. The Lagoon Theater opened in Uptown in 1913. The theater later changed its name to the Uptown Theater in 1929. In 1928 the Granada Theater opened in Uptown, providing an elaborate atmospheric setting in which to enjoy the newest movie theater technologies. The Granada's name was changed to the Suburban World in 1954. In the 1990s Landmark Theaters, the current owners of the Uptown Theater, opened a new theater complex located on Lagoon. In a nod to its earlier predecessor, this theater is named the Lagoon.

Another significant center of entertainment during the 1920s through the 1950s was the Minneapolis Arena. The arena, located at 29th and Dupont, drew more than 80,000 people to Uptown every year. The arena was the birthplace of Shipstad and Johnson's famous Ice Follies. The arena was also the home rink for the Minneapolis Millers, a minor league hockey team. During the summer, the ice surface was removed and roller skaters filled the space. On weekend evenings an orchestra played while couples danced on the large dance floor.

Uptown also offered several bowling alleys, the Dudley Riggs Brave New Workshop comedy theater, and several nightclubs and ballrooms. Seasonal entertainment included the Uptown Art Fair and the Aquatennial.

The Granada Theater is pictured here in 1928 shortly before it opened for business. The theater was designed by local architect Jack Liebenberg. Liebenberg also designed Temple Israel, a large neighborhood synagogue completed in 1927. His success at controlling the acoustics at Temple Israel led to his Granada Theater commission. Liebenberg later led the construction and renovation of hundreds of Midwestern movie theaters at the request of Paramount Pictures. The Granada Theater changed its name to Suburban World Theater in 1954. At that time, further remodeling was done, including adding the removal of the theater's wrought-iron doors and chandelier. (Courtesy Minneapolis Public Library.)

The 1920s were a golden age for large, ornate movie palaces. The Granada Theater, located on Hennepin Avenue, typified this new style of building. The theater's grand Moorish theme featured an atmospheric ceiling with stars and moving clouds and a spotlighted moon. The walls were lined with simulated plaster balconies, statues, and other touches meant to evoke romantic images of Spanish villas. (Courtesy Minneapolis Public Library.)

The Uptown Theater, located at the corner of Hennepin and Lagoon, changed its name from the Lagoon Theater in 1929 as part of a movement to give the Hennepin-Lake commercial district the name "Uptown." The theater shown here suffered severe fire damage in 1939 and was rebuilt in its current style, designed by local architects Liebenberg and Kaplan. The Clausen School of Dancing, also visible in this photograph, moved to its location above the Uptown Theater in 1931 and provided training for many neighborhood residents. The marquee of Uptown's other movie theater, the Granada, is visible farther up the street. (Courtesy Minnesota Historical Society.)

The Uptown Ballroom, located at Lake and Girard, offered live entertainment to its clientele. The building itself had been built as a movie theater. The Uptown area was one of Minneapolis's prime destinations for restaurants and entertainment during much of the twentieth century, and the Uptown Ballroom was just one of several neighborhood nightspots. The Uptown Ballroom building has recently returned to its entertainment roots after many years serving as a dental academy. (Courtesy Minneapolis Public Library.)

This Minneapolis versus Saint Paul hockey game, played in 1925 during the Kiwanians' National Convention, was just one of many events held at the Minneapolis Arena at 29th and Dupont. The ice skating season typically lasted from October through April, during which time hockey, figure skating, and public skating shared time. During the summer season the ice surface was dismantled and the surface used for roller skating. During the late 1920s and early 1930s the arena hosted weekly dance nights during the summer months. A 17-piece orchestra was broadcast live via WCCO radio while dancers enjoyed what was perhaps the nation's largest dance floor. During roller skating nights and during the ice skating season, patrons enjoyed the music of a large Wurlitzer pipe organ. Seating capacity for the arena was 5,500, and arena manager Lyle Wright estimated that that events drew 80,000 visitors annually. (Courtesy Minnesota Historical Society.)

Shown here are former hockey star and Minneapolis Miller coach Ching Johnson with the Lake Street Boosters group. The Minneapolis Arena and its many varied activities brought large numbers of people to the Uptown area every year. (Courtesy Minneapolis Public Library.)

Shipstad and Johnson's famous Ice Follies were born at the Minneapolis Arena at the urging of rink manager Lyle Wright. Many of the skaters came from the Minneapolis area, and the Follies returned every year to perform at their birthplace. The skaters in this production number "Enchanted Lake," were described by the Ice Follies as "ballet and beauty combined." This skating number was one of 18 acts in the 1954 Ice Follies show. (Courtesy Hennepin History Museum.)

Betty Schalow was featured in "A Most Unusual Wedding" in the 1952 Ice Follies. (Courtesy Hennepin History Museum.)

In 1958, former circus performer Dudley Riggs brought his Instant Theater Company to Café Espresso on University Avenue. In 1961 Brave New Workshop was added to the name. The theater moved to its 2605 Hennepin location in 1965. The price of admission in 1965 was $2. In 1998 the main stage was moved to Calhoun Square, although the 2605 Hennepin space remains in use. Brave New Workshop is now the United States' oldest ongoing satirical comedy theater. Pictured here are Tom Sherohman and an unidentified cast member in the late 1960s. (Courtesy Brave New Workshop.)

The 1970–1971 Dudley Riggs Brave New Workshop cast are shown here performing in "CHARLIE!, Or Mansion Ate Grapes." From left to right are Chris Tingley, Wick Howard, Jeff McLaughlin, Bo Kaprall, and Sid Strong. (Courtesy Brave New Workshop.)

This photograph, taken c. 1970, shows some young area residents and their motorcycles. The three Olson brothers lived at 3038 Emerson; this photograph was taken in their alley. Many of their neighborhood friends at the time rode motorcycles, and a popular pastime was cruising Lake Street or driving to nearby "Honda Hill" in Saint Louis Park near 36th Street and Highway 100. (Courtesy Terry and Tom Olson.)

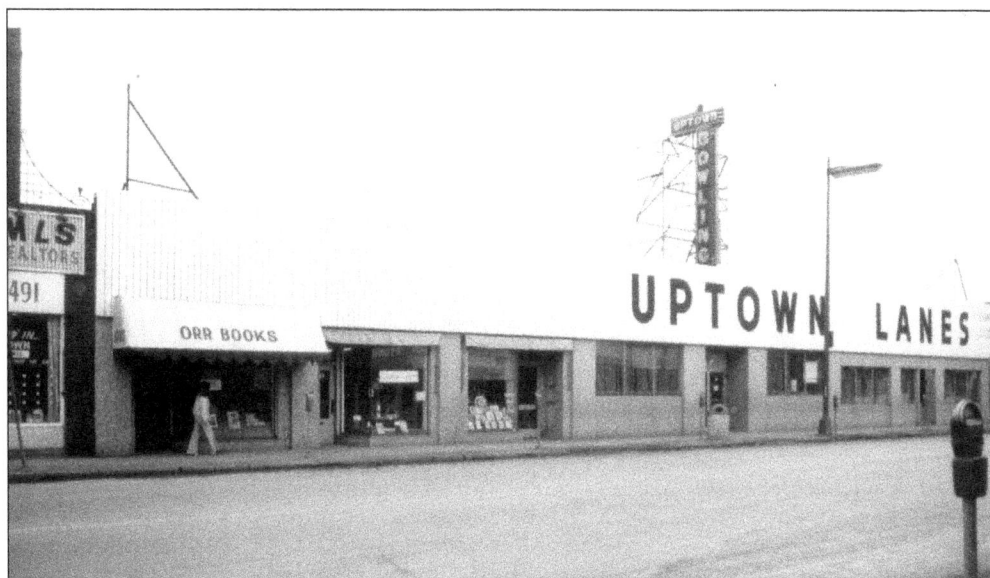

The Uptown Lanes bowling alley opened on Hennepin Avenue in 1939. It was owned and operated by Claude and Sis Kenady from 1947 until its closing in 1982. The alley purchased automatic pinsetters in 1958, their all-time busiest year. The alley was popular with league bowlers; among others were the Saturday morning blind league bowlers. (Courtesy Ray Harris.)

The first Uptown Art Fair was held in 1964 and featured 146 artists. It was sponsored by the Uptown Commercial Club as a way to bring business and attention to the Uptown business district. The Minneapolis Institute of Art helped with the planning of the first Uptown Art Fair. The fair has been organized by several organizations in the past. In 1985 the Uptown Association instituted a new juried artist selection process. The Uptown Art Fair has continued to grow in both size and quality, and is held annually in August. (Courtesy Ray Harris.)

www.ingramcontent.com/pod-product-compliance
Lightning Source LLC
Chambersburg PA
CBHW050606110426
42813CB00008B/2470